The
Postbus
Handbook

British Bus Publishing

Contents

The Postbus Handbook

FOREWORD BY DAVID GIBSON, ROYAL MAIL ROAD TRANSPORT STRATEGY

Royal Mail operates a unique network of Postbus passenger services through some of the most beautiful and remote parts of the UK. Postbuses combine the delivery and collection of mail with stops en route to pick up and set down passengers; they also provide an opportunity to explore the countryside in the company of local people.

Since the first postbus in 1967, a 220-strong postbus fleet has developed forming a key part of the Royal Mail national network, which handles in total 70 million letters a day, delivering to all addresses throughout the country - no matter how remote. The postbus is greatly valued in the rural areas it serves, as it provides a vital link for local communities, especially where there is no other means of public transport.

The postbus would not be the same without its drivers and the affection in which the service is held by the public is a tribute to them. Their enthusiasm, commitment and professionalism is typified by their "Mail must get through" attitude, no matter what the weather.

We look forward to the continued development of the postbus network, particularly at this time with new challenges being set by the Government's Integrated Transport Policy.

Finally, may I thank the Post Office Vehicle Club for their excellent work in documenting Royal Mail vehicle operations and long may they continue to do so.

Acknowledgements:

We are grateful to Martin Robinson for his article on tickets and publicity material produced by the Post Office. We would also like to express our thanks to many staff employed by the Post Office, including the Divisional Postbus Managers (especially Ken Ross in Scotland and Jack Wahlberg in the South East), the Vehicle Allocation Manager of Post Office Vehicle Services and to many Road Transport Workshop Managers and Delivery Office Managers throughout the country for their assistance over many years. The section on the history of the individual routes is derived from the Ride the Royal Mail Postbus newsletter of the Postbus Appreciation Society.

To keep the fleets up to date, information is made available to the PSV Circle on postbus and crewbus vehicles and this is published in the British Journal news-sheet. More in-depth information on postbuses, can be obtained from the publications of the Post Office Vehicle Club (see inside back cover) and the Postbus Appreciation Society (address: Bridge House, Bridestowe, OKEHAMPTON, Devon, EX20 4EL.).

The front cover photograph features the Leek postbus at Watton village in May 1995. *(M W Skillten).*

Contents correct to October 1998

ISBN 1 897990 47 2
Published by *British Bus Publishing Ltd*
The Vyne, 16 St Margarets Drive, Wellington,
Telford, TF1 3PH. *Telephone 01952 255669; Fax 07070 660418*

Introduction

Britain was a postal pioneer, being the first country to issue postage stamps and the first to introduce unified postage rates regardless of distance, however it was some sixty years behind other European countries such as Switzerland and Austria in introducing Postbuses. Indeed, by 1930 the yellow-liveried Saurers of the Swiss Postal administration were carrying some 3 million passengers a year. There is a fundamental difference, however, between our Postbuses and those of continental Europe. Ours are small passenger carrying vehicles used for mail delivery and collection on suitable routes in place of a van and covering the same duties, not for profit but as a service to the community. Postbuses in the rest of Europe are much larger, in some cases articulated vehicles for up to seventy passengers and their luggage plus mail, operate on main routes and only carry mail between Post Offices for onward delivery. The Post Office has a statutory duty to deliver letters, currently around 70 million each day, six days a week to every one of 26 million addresses from Land's End to John O'Groats.

In Britain the Post Office has its origins in the King's private network of couriers on horseback carrying his messages between 'Posts' at regular intervals on the roads radiating from London. It was opened to the public in 1635 by King Charles and an Act of Parliament in 1656 established a formal postal system. The first stage coaches ran in 1658 and John Palmer of Bath convinced the Government in 1782 that the privately operated network could carry mail as well as passengers. Radial routes were operated out of London each evening to important cities such as York and Bristol transferring mail en-route to riders on horseback and foot messengers who would take the Cross Posts to remote destinations. With the advent of the railways in the mid- nineteenth century this quickly became the preferred method of transport of both mail and passengers, the last mail coach running in 1898.

Daily delivery of letters by postmen on foot and bicycle was introduced in 1897. In 1903 a Stores Transport Department was established, under the control of Major C. Wheeler, OBE, the first vehicle to be purchased being a Wallis and Steevens traction engine in 1905. Mail transport, however, was still mainly carried out by contractors using both horse-drawn and motorised transport, although by 1909 more than five thousand postmen were using bicycles and carrier-tricycles to Major Wheeler's specification. Pedal cycles were not popular in hilly terrain and in 1914 the Engineer-in-Chief requested Treasury approval for the purchase of four motor cycle combinations.

After the war, the GPO experimented with ex-WD Fords, followed by the purchase of the first new mailvans in 1920. Motorisation expanded considerably during the 1920s and 1930s, initially using Ford vans and BSA motor cycle combinations and later Morris or Morris Commercial vans and the use of contractors gradually declined. However, McNamara & Co. continued to run a fleet of Morris mailvans from the General Post Office in London until nationalisation, and in some of the more remote areas of Scotland contractors continued to transport both mail and people. These tended to be real buses with mail carried in a separate compartment, in the livery of famous companies such as Highland Omnibuses and David MacBrayne, who also operated steamers between the Islands. The driver of the Sutherland Transport and Trading service between Lairg and Scourie, 'Red' Angus Mackenzie, wore a bus driver's jacket but his cap bore the GPO badge, he carried a mail pouch and was entrusted to empty letter boxes at the roadside. As a Royal Mail contract driver he sorted the mail at Lairg, made deliveries and cleared letterboxes along the route and also carried bagged mail, while on his own account he delivered newspapers and groceries to remote farms. Today's postbuses continue this tradition of service to rural communities, delivering meat, milk, groceries and prescriptions..

J. Harper & Sons at Blairgowrie operated two seven-seat Austin K8VC mail buses on routes to Braemar and Strathardle. CGS621 was replaced in 1962 by a Ford Thames registered RGS836 which was sold with the route to A. & C. McLennon, from whom the Post Office took over in 1978. *Robert Grieves collection*

The Experiments

In the early nineteen sixties the Government commissioned a study into the possible development of rural bus services in view of the declining network of existing routes and the closure of railway branch lines under the Beeching plan, mainly as a result of the growth in the use of private cars. The demand for rural transport is difficult to satisfy, being scattered and relatively small, however it has increased due to the closure of local facilities such as schools, shops and hospitals. The Committee on Rural Bus Services, chaired by D.T. Jack, carried out studies of British and some European rural bus services for the Ministry of Transport between 1959 and 1961. Although it ruled out the Swiss-style long-distance Postbus network for Britain, one proposal to arise from The Jack Report was for the General Post Office to investigate the possibility of carrying passengers with the mail in rural areas where this could be arranged without competing with existing bus operators or detriment to the mail collections and deliveries.

The GPO, then directly controlled by Central Government, was obliged to provide a daily delivery service to rural areas which provided little income but required a large investment in staff and vans. If the same vehicle and driver could provide for both mail and passengers then a basic bus service could be provided at little additional cost. Careful research was carried out to determine possible locations for the experimental Postbus services, such that all four are still operating thirty years later. The civil servants stirred into action and after trial journeys at the beginning of the year, the first Postbus service commenced operation on 20th February 1967 in a very rural part of mid-Wales, much of the route being around 600ft above sea level and the bus called at isolated hill-farms up steep and stony tracks with several gates to open and shut.

The bus was based at the Post Office in the small town of Llanidloes at the confluence of the rivers Wye and Severn, which had developed from weaving to light industries, and served Llangurig some five miles away, a former lead mining village on the A44 to Aberystwyth. The initial route was subjected to some criticism in the local newspaper, The Montgomeryshire Express by the Sub-postmaster at Llangurig, Wilfred Jones, who was also Chairman of Montgomeryshire County Council. He argued that "The bus will travel from Llanidloes in the morning with mail but will not pick up passengers until it has covered about 25 miles and has reached Llangurig on its way back to Llanidloes. It will call at farms but no passengers can board. It will go right up to Manod and four miles down the Rhayader road but not for passengers. In the summer people living in Llanidloes have to travel to Llangurig to meet the Aberystwyth to London bus but they won't be able to come out in the mail bus. I welcome the experiment but its great weakness is that the bus will not be carrying passengers over sections of the road where it is most needed."

In response the Director of Wales and Border Counties Postal Region said that it would be inconvenient for passengers to board the bus at 7am when it set out from Llanidloes on its delivery run which ended about noon at Llangurig. The five-mile return journey commenced at 12.15pm and only took 15 minutes, while the second passenger-carrying journey left Llanidloes at 4.15pm and the adult return fare was 2s 11d.

During the summer of 1967 locations for other routes were investigated - several were projected in Devon and Cornwall, one each in Stainmore in Westmoreland, County Durham, Derbyshire and East Anglia but all came to nothing. Alderman Jones' comments appear to have been heeded, however, as on 2nd October 1967 the Llanidloes service was retimed to give a 7am start and re-routed along both banks of the River Wye. Five further Morris J2s were converted at Coseley CRD in 1967 and the second service commenced from Honiton to Luppitt on 23rd October followed quickly by one from Penrith to Martindale on 30th October. However the service planned for Scotland encountered problems and it was not until 4th June 1968 that an alternative route commenced between Dunbar and Innerwick in East Lothian. The four routes were allowed to settle down and were watched carefully by Postal Headquarters during the proving period. Two of the six buses were employed as National Reserves, being used wherever required to cover for vehicles undergoing maintenance, for publicity purposes and also for route testing in preparation for further services. The experimental services were not an instant success and generally ran at a substantial loss but gave rural communities a valued lifeline, and as in so many large organisations once established they were allowed to continue.

The first Postbus to enter revenue-earning employment was Morris J2 KVB103D (105827) on 20th February 1967 on a route from Llanidloes to Llangurig. It is seen in its original livery and was, in common with other mailvans in Wales, given bilingual lettering in 1969. *G. Stain*

The Postbuses

Before describing the individual vehicles, for those not conversant with Post Office operations, it should be noted that the majority of mailvans are allocated to specific duties which often remain unchanged throughout the vehicles' lives. Local duty numbers, known as running numbers, are allocated at many delivery offices and these are carried on the individual vehicles. Exceptions are the reserve vehicles, generally based on individual Road Transport Workshops, and used to substitute regular vehicles when they are out of service for routine maintenance. Reserves generally carry running numbers incorporating the letter R. Postbuses are treated the same as other mailvans by the Post Office and are allocated to specific duties corresponding to individual postbus services.

Another feature of GPO operations was that most vehicles were subject to thorough periodic overhauls, not dissimilar to the policy adopted by London Transport with its buses. As a result, a number of Central Repair Depôts (CRDs) were set up by the GPO at Kidbrooke in south-east London, Yeading in west London, at Corby, Coseley near Wolverhampton and Bamber Bridge to undertake this work. The CRDs have played a significant part in the postbus story with conversion work carried out at most of them over the years. In the 1981 division of the Post Office, the CRDs at Yeading and Coseley transferred to British Telecom. The need for CRDs has diminished as vehicle lives have been reduced and all the CRDs have been closed in recent years. The site at Bamber Bridge near Preston was replaced by a smaller site at Chorley in 1993 and this continued the tradition of undertaking postbus conversion work until it, too, was deemed redundant in 1997.

A term which perhaps needs explanation in the following list is vehicle pools. A feature of GPO and Post Office operations was that vehicles were often delivered to workshops with sufficient space to store vehicles which were later allocated on an individual basis to replace time-expired vehicles or as additional vehicles. In the early days, postbuses tended to be ordered in advance of being required for new services and these vehicle pools were an important part of the early postbus story. Two vehicle pools in Scotland, Falkirk and Lockerbie, also undertook some conversion and modification work on postbuses, there being no CRD in Scotland.

The GPO started a system of fleet numbers, known as serial numbers, when the first mailvans were bought in 1920. This was a progressive system and had reached 100000-105978 by the time the first postbus was bought in 1966. The 1967

Opposite, top: **Of the twenty Dodge Postbuses ordered in 1977, ten went to Scotland, one to Wales and nine to England. YBB576T (7750046) served the Alnwick-Alwinton route all its life, and typifies the restyled front applied to the re-badged Commer body shell.** *Photobus Eckersley*

Opposite, bottom:- **Two of Sutherland Transport and Trading's attractive white and red mail buses outside Lairg Post Office in the early 1970s. Both 534BGD and NS4745 are Bedford J4LZ1s with 16-seat Duple Midland bodies featuring a large mail compartment at the rear. 534BGD dates from December 1960 and NS4745 from September 1961.** *Photobus Richardson*

deliveries had numbers in the next sequence, which ran from 220800-230795. In 1971, the Post Office introduced a new system for mailvans based on a seven digit serial number, the first denoting the year of purchase, the next two the type of vehicle and the last four a progressive number for each series starting at 0001. Type code 75 was allocated to personnel carriers and postbuses. Existing vehicles were renumbered in 1974 into the new system by using the last four numbers of the old serial with the first three numbers of the new system. Changes of use of individual vehicles often resulted in re-coding (of the second and third digits) or complete renumbering of the vehicle.

There was another renumbering in November 1980 when the postbus and personnel carrier type code was split up with 75 retained only for 11-seat postbuses, estate car postbuses became 76, Land Rovers code 77 and non-psv personnel carriers became type code 78. Again existing vehicles were changed and some postbuses relegated to crewbus duties were re-coded 78. The Land Rover serial story is quite involved with vehicles sometimes ordered as mailvans (code 10) converted to postbuses (code 75, later 77) and vice-versa, sometimes used as dual-purpose reserves and often relegated to workshop runabouts which often entailed another change of code to 80. Other codes which play a part in the story are codes 72-74 on cars (small, medium and large) and code 86 used briefly in 1980s for larger 16-seat postbuses.

Registration policy has varied over the years, in GPO days vehicles were registered centrally in London, normally in complete registration series reserved for the GPO. The formation of the Post Office in October 1969 led to registration being devolved to local Head Postmasters. Registration of new vehicles is now undertaken by suppliers on behalf of the Post Office to minimise the time needed to prepare a new vehicle for service.

Administration of postbuses and their routes has been carried out at regional level from the early 1970s. When the Post Office was formed, the GPO regional structure was retained and the regions were Scotland, Northern Ireland, Wales & the Marches (Wales & Border Counties until 1969), North Eastern, North Western, Midland, South Western, South Eastern, Eastern and London. This structure lasted until October 1986 when the Post Office was restructured into three operating divisions, Royal Mail Letters, Royal Mail Parcels (later known as Parcelforce) and Post Office Counters Ltd. The Royal Mail Letters operation was then organised around four Letters Territories (Northern, Eastern, Western and London) with District Head Postmasters. April 1992 saw a further change when the territories and districts were scrapped and nine new divisions (Scotland & Northern Ireland, North Wales & North West, North East, Midlands, Anglia, South Wales & South West, South Central, South East and London).

Throughout this handbook mailvans are referred to by their capacity in cubic feet (cf) and this reflects the official classification used by the Post Office. The vehicle tabulations show the dates the postbus was used in service, rather than the date registered and taxed or the date sold. Often postbuses for new services were delivered and taxed but not used on postbus duties for some months while the route was licensed and the drivers trained on the vehicles.

1966 / 67

The first Postbus service commenced operation in February 1967 based at Llanidloes in mid-Wales. A petrol-engined Morris J2M16 minibus was converted at Yeading CRD into a seven-seat postbus by adding a 30 cubic foot mail locker at the rear, the top of which formed a shelf for passengers' luggage. The total cost of the vehicle, including conversion, was £650. The Morris J2 was well known to the GPO with over nine-thousand vans bought for the green Post Office telephones fleet and about seventy-five as crewbuses. The equivalent mailvan at the time was the smaller Morris J4 10/12cwt. but this was considered unsuitable for use as a postbus. The vehicle carried the standard red livery with the traditional curved ROYAL MAIL lettering in gold leaf over the Queen's cypher.

During the summer of 1967 locations for other routes were investigated and five further Morris J2M16 petrol-engined minibuses were bought and sent to Coseley CRD for conversion in June 1967. Two were ready to enter service in October 1967 and started new routes at Penrith and Honiton but the route in Scotland met with problems and did not start until June 1968. The two remaining Morris' were retained as National Reserves, a most unusual arrangement, being used to substitute the other postbuses for maintenance, for publicity purposes and also for route testing in preparation for further services.

Following the success of the Llanidloes route, five more J2s were bought and numbered 226453-7. The first two were National Reserves and used on trials at a number of diverse locations, while the last two both inaugurated services, one from Honiton, the other from Dunbar. NYV974E (226455) is pictured, with the later style double-line lettering, at its base at Penrith. *G. Stain*

105827 had already been replaced by the time the 1974 renumbering was applied to vehicles while 226453-226457 became 7756453-7756457. Two of the J2s found further use as crewbuses while another was used as a driver-trainer at Edinburgh. The original postbus was replaced on 28th August 1974 after 120,241 miles and was sold in November 1974 to a private owner and was noted in Chorlton-cum-Hardy in May 1975. Scotland's first postbus found further use with the Sports and Social Association of Edinburgh Post Office and unsuccessful attempts were made by the Scottish Postal Board to persuade the Glasgow Transport Museum to acknowledge its place in history and accept it for preservation.

105827 Morris J2M16 7-seat postbus (Yeading CRD conversion)
226453-226457 Morris J2M16 7-seat postbus (Coseley CRD conversion)

serial	registration	chassis no.	location	route	in	out
105827	KVB103D	156363	Llanidloes	Llanidloes-Llangurig	2/67	8/74
226453	NYV972E	163449	National Reserve	at Bootle	3/68	6/69
				Honiton-Luppitt	9/69	10/69
				Llanidloes-Llangurig	12/69	2/70
				Honiton-Luppitt	8/70	10/70
				at Birmingham	3/71	8/71
				Penrith-Martindale	8/71	11/71
				Honiton-Luppitt	11/71	5/72
				Penrith-Martindale	5/72	8/72
				Canterbury-Crundale	9/72	2/73
				Billesdon services	5/73	2/74
				Honiton-Luppitt	2/74	11/74
				at Hereford	5/75	5/75
				Louth-Goulceby	5/75	10/75
			Liverpool	crewbus	10/75	3/79
226454	NYV973E	163453	National Reserve	Penrith-Martindale	8/68	9/68
				Llanidloes-Llangurig	9/68	2/69
				Penrith-Martindale	2/69	10/69
				Dunbar-Innerwick	10/70	12/70
				Llanidloes-Llangurig	12/70	1/71
				at Birmingham	8/71	9/72
				at Edinburgh	9/72	1/73
				at Newport, Mon.	1/73	11/73
				at Diss	11/73	1/74
				Llanidloes-Llangurig	1/74	5/74
				Billesdon services	5/74	7/76
226455	NYV974E	163452	Penrith	Penrith-Martindale	10/67	
				reserve	7/74	5/76
226456	NYV975E	163448	Honiton	Honiton-Luppitt	10/67	
			Southampton	crewbus	8/74	6/75
226457	NYV976E	163447	Dunbar	Dunbar-Innerwick	6/68	3/73
			Edinburgh	driver-trainer		3/77

1969/70

Two batches of Land Rover diesel 60cf. mailvans were purchased in 1969/70 - 272102-272124 in 1969 and 276720-276759 in 1970. Two from each batch were later converted to 4-seat dual-purpose reserves, able to substitute for both mailvans or for postbuses. In the 1974 renumbering, the vehicles became 9102102-9102124 and 0106720-0106759 and 272104 was further renumbered as a postbus around August 1977 as 9752104 but later reverted to mailvan serial 9102104. One of a batch of ten Morris 1800s, 281907 by then renumbered 0731907, was used on the Aboyne service in 1976.

272102-272124			Land Rover 88" 60cf. mailvan (*4-seat dual-purpose postbus)			
276720-276759			Land Rover 88" 60cf. mailvan (*4-seat dual-purpose postbus)			
281899-281908			Morris 1800 saloon			

serial	registration	chassis no.	location	route	in	out
272104*	KJS796H	27112144G	Lairg	reserve	2/70	
			Kylesku	mailvan		9/72
			Altnaharra	mailvan	9/72	6/74
			Dalwhinnie	mailvan	by 6/75	8/75
			Galashiels	dual-purpose reserve	9/75	c7/78
			Lockerbie	dual-purpose reserve	by 10/78	4/81
272115*	MST717J	27112311G	Tomatin	mailvan	5/70	
			Huntly	mailvan	by 5/75	by 10/75
			Kyle of Lochalsh	dual-purpose reserve	by 6/76	4/77
276720*	OST267J		Lairg	reserve	8/70	
			Lairg	dual-purpose reserve	c5/77	9/80
			Thurso	workshop van	10/80	
276743*	WSM950J		New Abbey	mailvan	-/71	
			Colonsay	mailvan	12/73	
			Oban	dual-purpose reserve	by 5/79	
281907	ORG827H		Aberdeen	Head Postmaster's car	-/70	
			Aboyne	Aboyne-Logie Coldstone	-/76	

Land Rover KJS796H (9752104) was fitted with seats at Lockerbie workshop for use as a dual-purpose reserve when required. It is seen here after demotion to workshop duties at Lockerbie workshop in September 1979.
P Walton

13

1971

In 1971, two small and two large crewbuses were bought: 1750001 a BMC 250JU 12-seat minibus for use by Giro (then part of the Post Office) at Liverpool and 1750002, a Land Rover 109″ station wagon for the Post Office's Staff College at Rugby. The larger buses were both subsequently converted to PSV standard and used as postbuses. 1760001 was a Leyland Terrier with Lex-SMB B24F bodywork also for Rugby Staff College. The double nearside seat ahead of the entrance was removed before it was PSV certified as B23F in July 1974. It was sent to Islay where it initially operated the Islay to Portnahaven service and later the Laide to Achnasheen route with the seating further reduced to B17F with additional mail accommodation.

1760002 was a heavier Leyland Boxer with a longer version of the Lex-SMB body with B44F seating, which was bought to replace 201766, a Bedford SBG with Mulliner B31F bought second-hand in November 1966 from the Ministry of Defence and reregistered KVB673D. 1760002 was delivered new to Kidbrooke in January 1972 and was sent to Camden garage in March 1972 but was not wanted and it remained unregistered until it was sent to Cardiff in December for use as a crewbus between the city centre and the newly opened Mechanised Letter Office in Penarth Road. Here it received the bilingual Welsh livery which had been introduced in 1969 as part of the Prince of Wales investiture celebrations. It returned to Kidbrooke in September 1975 before heading north to Lockerbie in May 1976 where it was modified to B20F (plus mail) and prepared for its Certificate of Fitness which it obtained at Edinburgh in August 1976, allowing it to replace its smaller brother on the Laide to Achnasheen route from 7th August. Two more Land Rover mailvans from a batch of thirty vehicles bought in 1971 were later converted to dual-purpose reserves.

1760001 was sold in October 1979 and became a mobile fish and chip shop in Falkirk from 1980 until at least February 1982. 1760002 was replace in April 1979, and stood at Kirkcaldy between August 1979 and March 1980 with its markings removed before being used for further use as a school bus. It was last noted licensed to December 1985.

1100001-1100030   Land Rover 88" 60cf. mailvan (*4-seat dual-purpose postbus)
1750001   BMC 250JU 12-seat personnel carrier
1750002   Land Rover 109" 12-seat personnel carrier
1760001   Leyland Terrier TR750 with Lex-SMB B24F bodywork
1760002   Leyland Boxer BX1000 with Lex-SMB B44F bodywork

serial	registration	chassis no.	location	route	in	out
1100003*	MSO794K	9060839A	Grantown-on-Spey	reserve	2/72	
			Grantown-on-Spey	dual-purpose reserve	by 2/76	5/81
1100012*	RST607K	9060848A	Dingwall	reserve	2/72	
			Dingwall	dual-purpose reserve	by 5/79	6/81
1750001	YKD385J	32668	Liverpool	Giro services	4/71	
			Birmingham	crewbus	12/71	2/80
1750002	EAC165K	28101435H	Rugby	Coton House staff college		
1760001	FNX580K	415515	Rugby	Coton House staff college	1/72	
			Islay	Islay-Portnahaven	7/74	
			Laide	Laide-Achnasheen	1/76	
			Inverness	Coton House staff college	8/76	4/79
1760002	CBO315L	416337	Cardiff	crewbus	12/72	9/75
			Laide	Laide-Achnasheen	8/76	4/79

Left:- **In the early days of Postbus development, various types and sizes of vehicles were tried out. Terrier FNX580K (1760001) with Lex-SMB bodywork had started life at the PO College in Rugby, but was in time allocated to the Islay-Portnahaven and Laide-Achnasheen routes, with its original capacity of 23 seats reduced to 17 plus mail. The Leyland Terrier was repainted into the new double-line livery but the boxer was not. It was photographed at Laide in August 1976.** *P Walton*

Far left:- **The larger Leyland Boxer CBO315L (176002) with Lex-SMB bodywork was initially used as a personnel carrier in Cardiff. It is here seen at Penarth Road in the spring of 1974 displaying the Welsh bilingual lettering.** *M D Street*

1972

The Morris J2 was no longer in production when the next routes were introduced and the petrol-engined Bedford CF with 106" wheel-base was initially chosen despite it not being common in the Post Office fleet. The decision was presumably made because minibus conversions were readily available from Martin Walter of Folkestone under the Dormobile name, although 2750001 was a local purchase in Scotland and was a 12-seat Utilabus that required down-seating and other modifications at Glasgow workshop to obtain a Certificate of Fitness. The six Bedford CFSs had a nine-seat layout with the rear doors used as the passenger entrance and the nearside cab door as the emergency exit, with an unguarded mail pen inside - not a very satisfactory arrangement. Two of the batch were delivered in green and cream, and they were repainted before entering service, the five in Scotland having a white roof and the traditional curved ROYAL MAIL in gold over the King's cypher centrally on the body sides. The last at Canterbury had a yellow roof and a new style of lettering - the words *Royal Mail Post Bus* in a large yellow double-line type face that was adopted for all mailvans from 1975, and some of the earlier Morris J2s were repainted into this scheme. The Canterbury bus ran a service to Curdle which had been inaugurated by one of the Morris J2s, but within weeks it had been demoted to a reserve, being replaced by one of the new Comers. The Bedfords had short lives as postbuses but 2750004 found further use as a crewbus (and survived long enough to be given crewbus serial 2780004 in 1980) while 2750006 was used as a mailvan with its seats removed and was renumbered 2170006, later being re-seated and used as

The 1972 order for Postbuses was split between Dormobile 9-seat psv conversions of Bedford CF vans and Commers with 11-seats. The last of the batch of six CFs was allocated to Canterbury as a Reserve bus, but the other five went to Scotland with XWS416K (2750001) being photographed at the far end of the route from Elgol to Broadford on the Isle of Skye. *Vauxhall Motors Ltd*

a publicity van with serial 2750006 restored. 2750002/3 both found further use as school buses with Sinclair of West Sinness. The unsatisfactory layout of the Bedford CFS was resolved by changing to the Commer 2000LB, over six-thousand PB vans having entered service with the telephone fleet since 1965. The vehicle was popular with coach and private hire operators as it was readily available with PSV conversion by Rootes of Maidstone, incorporating a raised glass fibre roof with a central luggage well reached by folding steps behind the nearside cab door. A side door gave safer access to eleven seats, which were separated from the driver and mail by a full-height screen with a hole in it to allow passengers to hand their fares to the driver. A capacious area for mail occupied the space normally taken by the front passenger seat with loading through the nearside cab door. Nine petrol-engined Commers were delivered between October and December 1972 and the model quickly became the standard postbus, not only being more suitable for stage carriage work but also more economical to operate than the Bedfords. The livery followed that of the Bedfords with yellow roofs and lettering in England, and white roofs and traditional markings in Scotland.

The Commers also had comparatively short lives and were replaced by later Commers and Dodges not required to start new routes. 2750012 found further use as a postal engineering crewbus from August 1977 and was repainted in red with a white band with serial number 2560012. 2750010 found further use with the Edinburgh Staff Association and later operated for General & Domestic Appliances of South Queensferry.

2750001　　　　　　Bedford CFS 9-seat postbus (Dormobile/Glasgow workshop conversion)
2750002-2750006　　Bedford CFS 9-seat postbus (Dormobile conversion)
2750007-2750015　　Commer 2000LB 11-seat postbus (Rootes conversion)

serial	registration	chassis no.	location	route	in	out
2750001	XWS416K	842600	Elgol	Elgol-Broadford	4/72	
			Lochboisdale	reserve	2/73	12/76
2750002	YSG487K	613465	Galashiels	Galashiels-Lilliesleaf	8/72	6/73
			Ardgay	Ardgay-Strathoykel	7/73	12/76
2750003	YWS948K	616955	Lochmaddy	Lochmaddy-Solas/Benbecula	6/72	5/73
			Strathconon	Strathconon-Muir of Ord-Tomich	6/73	
			Lochinver	Lochinver-Drumbeg	1/74	12/76
2750004	AFS386K	615459	Kylesku	Kylesku-Elphin	9/72	
			Toscaig	Toscaig-Applecross	6/75	
			Motherwell	crewbus	6/76	by 8/80
2750005	AFS387K	615609	Castlebay	Castlebay-Eoligarry	8/72	4/77
2750006	XUF902K	616978	Canterbury	Canterbury-Crundale	10/72	
			Canterbury	reserve	12/72	8/77
			Polegate	mailvan	4/78	
			Brighton	Regional RPO	c6/79	10/82
2750007	BSC494L	153286	Craignure	Craignure-Lochbuie	12/72	
			Oban	reserve	4/76	2/77
2750008	BSF96L	154559	Cupar	Cupar-Peat Inn	12/72	1/77
2750009	BSF97L	153990	Tigharry	Tigharry-Lochmaddy	12/72	5/77
2750010	CSC89L	154500	Dunbar	Dunbar-Innerwick	3/73	10/78
2750011	BSG95L	154442	Skerray	Skerray-Tongue	1/73	5/77
2750012	BSG672L	154583	Lockerbie	Lockerbie-St. Anns/Hightae	4/73	1/77
			Glasgow	postal engineering crewbus	8/77	11/80
2750013	BSG644L	154610	Elgol	Elgol-Broadford	2/73	12/76
2750014	BSG673L	154790	Nairn	Nairn-Glenferness	2/73	
			Nairn	reserve	8/78	
			Aberdeen	crewbus	by 12/78	2/79
2750015	CCD532L	155269	Canterbury	Canterbury-Crundale	12/72	
			Canterbury	reserve	8/77	2/78

1973

A further forty-seven PSV-certified Commers were bought in 1973 in two contracts of twenty-eight and nineteen, most of the first batch featuring the metal steps up to the roof, and there were also three crewbuses for staff transport which were numbered in the same series. Commer 3750007 launched the Lochinver-Drumbeg service in July, however as this coastal route is exposed to high winds off the Atlantic, the postbus was found to be too light for the buffeting and it was exchanged for Bedford CFS 2750003 from the Strathconon route. Commer 3750019 was exhibited at the Scottish Motor Show at Glasgow in November 1973. 3750048-3750050 became 3780048-3780050 in the 1980 renumbering of crewbuses.

A 1972 Ford Transit long-wheelbase minibus was bought from Stewart of Aberfeldy with the service to Glenlyon when the owner retired in January 1974 and it was given serial 3750051. It was immediately replaced by a Commer and was sent to the Rugby Staff College before returning to Scotland for the summer service on Islay in March 1975 in place of the Leyland Terrier, ending its days at Glasgow with a white roof, a yellow band and some seats removed.

Successful as the Commer was proving, it became apparent that some routes in Scotland would require a smaller vehicle. In November 1973 the first Land Rover 88" postbus entered service fitted with four passenger seats in the load space, an emergency exit window in the roof (but no side windows), a white roof and the spare wheel mounted on the bonnet. Ten Land Rover diesel mailvans from a delivery of forty were proposed for conversion into postbuses at Falkirk workshop and it was intended that 3750052-3750058 would be converted from 3100001/4/5/6/8/9/11 and 3750060-3750062 from 3100034/33/35 but delays with the service at Lochindorb allowed 3100009 to be sent to Wales as a mailvan as an urgent replacement for an Austin Gipsy mailvan and the allocated serial 3750057 was left unused. In late 1976, three further mailvans (3100003/26/25) were converted at Fraserburgh workshop to dual-purpose reserves numbered 3750063-3750065 with white roofs and white wheels. 3750052/55/56/58/60/2 were further renumbered 3770052/55/56/58/60/2 in 1980, while 3750063/4 later reverted to their original mailvan serials 3100003/26. 3750065 eventually ended up as a workshop van at Galashiels and was renumbered 3800025 by August 1985.

Another conversion to a postbus involved one of a pair of Morris Marina estate cars 3560005 ordered to replace a 1967 Morris Oxford at Scotland's postal headquarters; it was used on a low-traffic route which did not justify a Land Rover. It was renumbered 3750059 and further renumbered 3760059 in 1980. The other one of the pair, new as 3560004 but renumbered 3730012 in 1976, was also used at Aboyne as a postbus in 1976.

Not all Postbuses operate in rugged scenery! Commer CCD532L (2750015), the last of the 1972 order of nine Commers, and the only one not to have gone to Scotland, is pictured preparing to leave Canterbury bus station for its trip to Crundale in 1975. *POVC collection*

3100001-3100040	Land Rover 88" 60cf. mailvan
3730012	Morris Marina 4-seat estate car
3750001-3750047	Commer PBCM2090P 11-seat postbus (Rootes conversion)
3750048-3750050	Commer PBCM2090L 13-seat personnel carrier (*11-seats)
3750051	Ford Transit 12-seat postbus (Deansgate conversion)
3750052-3750056	Land Rover 88" 4-seat postbus (Falkirk conversion)
3750057	serial not used
3750058	Land Rover 88" 4-seat postbus (Falkirk conversion)
3750059	Morris Marina 4-seat estate car postbus
3750060-3750062	Land Rover 88" 4-seat postbus (Falkirk conversion)
3750063-3750065	Land Rover 88" 4-seat postbus (Fraserburgh conversion)

serial	registration	chassis no.	location	route	in	out
3730012	PFS419M	MH5W914445	Edinburgh	postal-engineering	1/74	
			Aberdeen	npsv	11/76	
			Aboyne	Aboyne-Logie Coldstone	12/76	
			Aberdeen	npsv		10/79
3750001	DSC181L	160087	Lochmaddy	Lochmaddy-Solas/Benbecula	5/73	4/77
3750002	DSC182L	160083	Alligin	Alligin-Kinlochewe	6/73	2/77
3750003	DUF488L	160136	Dorking	Dorking-Ockley	8/73	9/78
3750004	DSC942L	160076	Scourie	Scourie-Laxford-Kylestrome	6/73	3/77
3750005	DSG804L	162050	Islay	Islay services	10/73	3/77
3750006	DSC943L	161529	Lairg	reserve	5/73	3/77
			Edinburgh	driver trainer	3/77	12/80
3750007	DSF749L	160072	Lochinver	Lochinver-Drumbeg	7/73	
			Strathconon	Strathconon-Muir of Ord-Tomich	1/74	1/77

3750008	DSF750L	161882	Melrose	Galashiels-Lilliesleaf	6/73	8/78
			Plymouth	crewbus	-/79	8/80
3750009	DSF751L	160929	Edinburgh	reserve	5/73	
			Lockerbie	reserve	11/74	6/78
3750010	DSG805L	162821	Islay	Islay services	10/73	
			Islay	crewbus	3/77	
			Stornoway	workshop vehicle	by 7/79	8/80
3750011	DSG806L	161724	Bettyhill	Bettyhill-Kinbrace	8/73	
			Castle Douglas	reserve	1/76	3/77
3750012	ECD641L	162847	Oxted	Oxted-Lingfield	9/73	9/78
3750013	NFS590M	162778	Islay	Islay services	10/73	3/77
3750014	NFS591M	163280	Thornhill	Thornhill-Moniaive	9/73	3/77
			Lockerbie	postal engineering	4/78	4/81
3750015	DSC944L	160096	Biggar	Biggar-Tweedsmuir	8/73	1/77
3750016	NCD242M	162052	Redhill	reserve	8/73	7/80
3750017	NEE492M	161092	Louth	Louth-Goulceby	11/73	8/78
3750018	NJF1M	163395	Billesdon-87	Billesdon services	9/73	11/78
3750019	OFS10M	161951	Port Ellen	reserve	12/73	11/78
3750020	NJF12M	163427	Billesdon-88	Billesdon services	9/73	11/78
3750021	NUF959M	164535	Petworth	Petworth-Bignor	3/74	2/80
			Crawley	crewbus	4/80	6/82
3750022	RTJ319M	164543	Broughton	Broughton-Cockley Beck	3/74	2/80
3750023	OFS252M	164547	Aberfeldy	Aberfeldy-Lawers	1/74	8/78
			Perth	crewbus	by 12/78	by 7/83
3750024	OSF241M	164572	Aberfeldy	Aberfeldy-Lubreoch	1/74	9/78
			Perrth-47	crewbus		by 8/80
3750025	OCD701M	164581	Hungerford-2	Hungerford-Great Shefford	7/74	11/80
3750026	OFS253M	164614	Anstruther	Anstruther-Arncroach	1/74	8/78
			Glenrothes	crewbus	by 2/79	3/80
3750027	NUF241M	164760	Sittingbourne	Sittingbourne-Wormshill	3/74	1/79
3750028	OFS254M	164817	Dingwall	reserve	11/73	12/76
3750029	OCD702M	173593	Hungerford-1	Hungerford-Lambourn	7/74	8/80
3750030	OCD703M	174690	Hungerford-R8	reserve	7/74	11/80
3750031	OSF757M	173609	Cupar	reserve	2/74	6/80
3750032	OSG708M	174664	Galashiels	reserve	2/74	3/80
			Haddington	Haddington-Garvald	3/80	6/80
3750033	PFS143M	175627	West Linton	West Linton-Romanno Bridge	8/74	
			Falkirk	reserve	1/76	6/80
3750034	PSC361M	175647	Castle Douglas	Castle Douglas-Corsock	8/74	7/78
3750035	OUF269M	175642	Tunbridge Wells	Tunbridge Wells-Mayfield	4/74	5/79
3750036	PSC362M	175620	Castle Douglas	Castle Douglas-Mossdale	8/74	8/78
3750037	RFS211M	176024	Kelso	Kelso-Stichill	10/74	11/78
3750038	PSC363M	176051	Haddington	Haddington-Garvald	6/74	3/80
3750039	PWC472M	175985	Diss	Diss-Gislingham	3/74	2/79
			High Wycombe-43	crewbus		c-/80
3750040	PWC473M	176041	Diss	reserve	3/74	3/80
3750041	RFS214M	176198	Kirriemuir	Kirriemuir-Glen Clova	9/74	6/78
3750042	OHH769M	176006	Penrith	Penrith-Martindale	7/74	
			Penrith	reserve	6/76	
			Barrow-in-Furness	reserve	5/79	8/79
3750043	RFS215M	176010	Hawick	Hawick-Bonchester Bridge	10/74	9/78
3750044	RFS212M	176063	Leven	Leven-New Gilston	3/75	10/78
3750045	RFS213M	174622	Lockerbie	reserve	8/74	12/75
3750046	RFS216M	176769	West Calder	West Calder-Tarbrax	8/74	4/79
			Bathgate	crewbus	by 2/80	9/80
3750047	RFS217M	177116	Aberfoyle	Aberfoyle-Kinlochard	1/75	1/80
3750048*	TMM469M	176623	London (SWDO).	crewbus	11/73	12/81
3750049	PKA689M	176587	Bootle-9BO	crewbus	2/74	3/82
3750050	GPU632N	181878	Southend-on-Sea	crewbus	10/74	
			Colchester	crewbus	11/80	5/82
3750051	UES86K	BC05MB58516	Rugby Staff College	crewbus and postbus reserve	1/74	3/75
			Port Ellen	reserve	6/75	1/77
			Glasgow-RMTO10	reserve	by 11/77	7/80
3750052	RFS219M	90604253A	Altnaharra	Altnaharra-Portnacon	6/74	8/80
3750053	XST149M	90604303A	Killilan	Killilan-Dornie	11/73	2/80
3750054	RFS218M	90604259A	Tomatin	Tomatin-Coignafearn	6/74	9/80
3750055	RFS220M	90604258A	Rogart	Rogart-Scibercross	10/74	8/81
3750056	OFS825M	90604305A	Ardgay	Ardgay-Craigs	6/74	8/81
3750058	SSC326N	90604255A	Kirriemuir	Kirriemuir-Glen Prosen	9/74	
			Bettyhill	Bettyhill-Kinbrace	1/76	11/80

The 1972 Ford Transit minibus UES86K (3750051) bought from Stewart of Aberfeldy in January 1974 was initially sent to the staff college at Rugby but later returned to Scotland, being used at Port Ellen as a reserve postbus for about eighteen months. It is pictured here at Portnahaven on Islay in September 1976.
B D Nicholson

3750059	NSC306M	MH5W914454	Edinburgh	car at Regional HQ	12/73	
			Melrose	Melrose-Maxton	1/75	
			Galashiels	reserve	4/75	
			Dunblane	Dunblane-Braco	9/76	3/78
			Falkirk	reserve (npsv)	4/78	5/81
3750060	GSX137N	90604137A	Gorthleck	Gorthleck-Killen Lodge	2/75	7/81
3750061	HFS618N	90604281A	Grantown-on-Spey	Grantown-Lochindorb	3/75	
			Lockerbie	reserve	5/80	
			Alford	mailvan	1/81	9/82
3750062	HFS621N	90604312A	Drumnadrochit	Drumnadrochit-Grotaig	6/75	9/81
3750063	YRS627M	90604261A	Glenkindie	mailvan	7/73	
			Alford	mailvan	6/76	
			Kelso	dual-purpose reserve	12/76	
			Peebles	Peebles-Manorhead	8/77	3/78
			Aberdeen	dual-purpose reserve	c6/78	8/82
3750064	YRG488L	90604256A	Alford	mailvan	7/73	
			Bressay	Isle of Bressay	12/76	
			Huntly	reserve	3/78	8/82
3750065	YRG489L	90604254A	Ballater	mailvan	7/73	
			Banchory	mailvan	6/74	
			Dollar	Dollar-Glendevon	11/76	
			Duns	Duns-Abbey St. Bathans	8/77	4/78
			Galashiels	reserve	c6/78	9/82
			Galashiels	workshop van	by 8/85	

The first estate car postbus, Morris Marina NSC306M (3750059), photographed on the Dunblane to Braco service at Braco in March 1977. It started life as a non-psv and finished as a non-psv, with postbus use at three locations in between. *P Walton*

Numerically the first Commer postbus, BSC494L (2750007) is seen meeting the ferry at Craignure, on Mull, in 1973. The later Commers and Dodges still had the raised roof, which had a sunken middle section for the stowage of luggage, but did not have the steps up the side visible in this shot. *G Stain*

1974

A further thirty Commers with Rootes conversions were delivered for new services and to replace three of the Morris J2s. 4750018 was later renumbered 4780018. Two more Commer crewbuses were bought for use in London; 4750032 became 4780032 in the 1980 renumbering while 4750031 was renumbered 4700031 in 1978 and then transferred to telephone fleet and renumbered again to 74 376 0050. Two pairs of Morris Marina estate cars were bought locally in Scotland for low-capacity services.

4750001-4750030	Commer PBCM2090P 11-seat Postbus (Rootes conversion)
4750031-4750032	Commer PBCM2090P 6-seat Personnel Carrier
4750033-4750036	Morris Marina 1.8 estate car 4-seat postbus

serial	registration	chassis no.	location	route	in	out
4750001	NAO201P	180248	Penrith	Penrith-Martindale	6/76	5/80
4750002	PUF484M	180226	Heathfield	Heathfield-Waldron	6/74	8/79
4750003	GSX136N	181211	Dingwall	Dingwall-Heights of Dochcarty	3/75	6/80
4750004	HFS625N	181223	Pitlochry	reserve	4/75	6/80
			Perth-47	crewbus	by 8/80	5/82
4750005	HFS626N	180276	Castle Douglas	Castle Douglas-Auchencairn	6/75	6/80
4750006	RSG213M	180154	Islay	Islay services	11/74	9/78
4750007	HFS627N	180414	Falkirk	Regional Reserve	-/74	
			Killin	Killin-Callander	11/75	4/79
4750008	PUF899M	181354	Hungerford	Hungerford-Kintbury	7/74	11/80
4750009	LFS946P	180788	Kyle of Lochalsh	reserve	10/75	8/80
4750010	OFO192N	181996	Llanidloes	Llanidloes-Llangurig	8/74	7/80
			Newtown	reserve		6/81
4750011	SCD323N	181970	Hungerford	reserve	7/74	c5/81
4750012	LFS955P	182619	Tiree	Isle of Tiree	11/75	4/80
4750013	LFS956P	182639	Aboyne	Aboyne-Logie Coldstone	1/76	8/80
			Aberdeen	crewbus		9/81
4750014	SCD325N	182913	Hailsham	Hailsham-Bodle Street Green	9/74	2/81
4750015	LFS957P	182852	Tarbert	Tarbert-Skipness	11/75	5/80
4750016	SCD327N	182988	Hailsham	reserve	9/74	5/81
4750017	MFS334P	183050	Glenluce	Glenluce-Stranraer	1/76	12/77
			Dunoon	Dunoon-Tighnabruaich	3/78	5/79
4750018	SCD331N	183016	Newport, IoW	Newport-Newtown	1/75	1/81
			Redhill	crewbus	by 8/82	2/83
4750019	HVW365N	183174	Colchester	Colchester-Flatford	9/75	11/80
			Harlow	crewbus		12/82
4750020	GAP157N	182984	Newport, IoW	reserve	1/75	6/81
4750021	GAP156N	183183	Petersfield	Petersfield-Froxfield	2/75	10/80
4750022	KJN394P	183706	Colchester	reserve	9/75	4/81
			High Wycombe	crewbus	7/81	5/82
4750023	GAP158N	183770	Newport, IoW	Newport-Brighstone	1/75	1/81
4750024	GFJ277N	184036	Honiton	Honiton-Luppitt	10/74	7/80
			Bath	crewbus		4/81
4750025	MFS344P	183853	Annan	Annan-Creca	1/76	4/78
			Lockerbie	reserve	by 7/78	7/80
4750026	MFS340P	183901	Lockerbie	Annan-Powfoot	11/75	7/80
4750027	GAP159N	184072	Newbury	Newbury-Brightwalton	8/75	8/81
4750028	MFS341P	184077	Lockerbie	Lockerbie-Hightae	11/75	4/78
			Castle Douglas	Castle Douglas-Corsock	7/78	7/80
4750029	GYJ812N	182327	Newbury	Newbury-West Ilsley	8/75	8/81

The relatively short run from Selkirk to Ashkirk in the Scottish Borders, introduced in 1975, was inaugurated by Marina estate GSX134N (4750033). At the time all Postbuses were numbered in the x75 series, type code x76 only being introduced for estate cars in November 1980. *Photobus Eckersley*

4750030	HYJ261N	183892	Eastbourne	reserve	8/75	
			Henley-on-Thames	reserve	5/76	3/79
4750031	GYU652N		London	International Telegraphs		
			London	International Automatic Services		
4750032	GYE865N	185313	London (Camden)	crewbus	10/74	12/83
4750033	GSX134N	MH5W9-28499M	Selkirk	Selkirk-Ashkirk	3/75	4/80
4750034	GSX133N	MH5W9-24336M	Applecross	Applecross-Toscaig	2/75	
			Kylesku	Kylesku-Elphin	6/75	6/77
4750034	HFS623N	MH5W9-29749M	Kelso	Kelso-Roxburgh	3/75	4/80
4750036	HFS624N	MH5W9-30771M	Melrose	Melrose-Maxton	4/75	4/78
			Galashiels	reserve		4/80

Opposite top:- **The 1974 order for Commer 11-seat Postbuses included three for the Lockerbie workshop area, two of which - MFS 340/4P (4750026/5) - are pictured in the corner of the Annan Delivery Office yard. The former spent all its working life on the Powfoot route, while the latter served on the Annan-Creca route before becoming the Lockerbie reserve bus.** *Photobus Eckersley*

Opposite, bottom:- **Commer GAP158N (4750023) on the Newport to Brighstone service showing the large yellow Royal Mail Post Bus lettering and yellow roof used on postbuses in England from 1972.** *D Hill*

1975

No less than eighty Commers were bought in 1975 anticipating the proposed expansion of services, the majority opening new routes and therefore registration was rather protracted, the last entering service in 1979 by which time others from the batch were reaching the end of their working lives as postbuses. Several vehicles were diverted from their intended allocations when routes failed to materialise such that Eastern and South Eastern Postal Regions were asked to send their pooled postbuses to Wales and the North East for new services. Eastern Postal Region had received 5750001/3 (sent to the North East), 5750007 (sent to Wales), 5750012/4/8/23/8 (sent to Liverpool for use as crewbuses), 5750030 (sent to Midlands) and South Eastern Postal Region had received 5750008/11/38/41/2 (sent to Wales) and 5750050 (sent to the Midlands).

5750013, intended for Henley-on-Thames, was hurriedly despatched from Maidstone pool to Honiton in October 1976 when 4750024 was damaged in an accident. The yellow double-line style was extended to Scotland with this delivery, incorporating an outline King's cypher and in contrast to English Post Buses were lettered 'Royal Mail Bus'. Eleven of the batch were new as crewbuses and carried the normal mailvan livery rather than the large Post Bus lettering, although retaining the yellow roof.

5750001 became 5780011 and 5750003/5/12/4/8/22/3/4/8/9/33/4/7 became 5780003/5/12/4/8/22/3/4/8/9/33/4/7 in the 1980 renumbering. 5750008 carried bilingual lettering on the cab doors indicating Welsh Office sponsorship of the route. 5750060, allocated to Lochboisdale, crashed in Glasgow on delivery in February 1977 and was broken up, and 5750073 from the same batch was diverted from Oban to replace it. 5750002 had a tough life - it covered over 70,000 miles in less than two years and was written off in an accident in April 1978. It was replaced on the Rothbury-Alwinton route by 5750001 which had spent thirty-three months in store at Ipswich after being delivered new to Kidbrooke in July 1975 for the usual photographs of the first of each delivery.

Two factory-produced Leyland Sherpa crewbuses with glazed rear doors and chromium-plated bumpers were also bought numbered 5750081/2, becoming 5780081/2 in 1980.

Another fifteen Morris Marina estate cars were bought locally by Scotland from British Leyland dealers in England and Scotland (5750087-91 from Stewart & Arden and 5750092-7 from Caffyns) and PSV-converted at Lockerbie for new services which did not justify an 11-seater. 5750095 was registered in anticipation of a service from Laide to Braemore which failed to materialise, finally entering service on the Bernera to Callanish route in April 1977.

Eight Land Rovers from a large order for sixty-five mailvans were PSV-converted at Lockerbie before entering service, the first five being the last to have the emergency exit in the roof. Their intended serials, 5100035-7/41-3/8/9 were replaced with 5750098-5750105. Three further conversions were undertaken at Falkirk later in the year and 5100007/11/39 became 5750106-8 in

A line of Commers, awaiting the repaint of roof and wheels to the white 'Scottish specification', form the backdrop to Marina estate postbus NSX878P (5750093) when newly allocated to the Lockerbie-Corrie Common route. *POVC collection*

order. 5750108 reverted to 5100039 to June 1978 while 5750098-5750107 were renumbered 5770098-5770107 in 1980. 5770100/7 were later further renumbered 5800100 and 5800011 on demotion on workshop vehicles. Two other mailvans from this batch later became dual-purpose reserves.

A petrol-engined Ford A0610 (numbered 5760001) with Tricentrol Unibus bodywork in dark blue with off-white window surrounds was bought for staff transport at Rugby Training College. It was renumbered 5780001 in 1980.

5100001-5100065	Land Rover 88" 60cf. mailvan (*4-seat dual-purpose postbus)
5750001-5750080	Commer PBCM2090P 11-seat Postbus (Rootes conversion) or
	(♦7-seats plus mail compartment)
5750081-5750082	Leyland Sherpa 240 12-seat personnel carrier
5750083-5750097	Morris Marina 4-seat estate car Postbus
5750098-5750105	Land Rover 88" 4-seat Postbus (Lockerbie conversion)
5750106-5750108	Land Rover 88" 4-seat Postbus (Falkirk conversion)
5760001	Ford A0610 with Tricentrol Unibus B25F bodywork

serial	registration	chassis no.	location	route	in	out
5100013*	TSE269R	90611221A	Grantown-on-Spey	mailvan	12/76	
			Grantown-on-Spey	dual-purpose reserve	6/80	
			Dalwhinnie	Dalwhinnie-Drummin	6/81	3/84
5100044*	KST95P	90611258A	Inverness	mailvan	1/76	
			Inverness	dual-purpose reserve		7/83

Fleet No	Reg	No	Location	Route/Notes	Date	Date
5750001	PVK471S	405263	Rothbury-4	Rothbury-Alwinton	6/78	4/82
			Wakefield	crewbus	4/82	4/84
5750002	JRG132P	405301	Rothbury	Rothbury-Alwinton	11/75	4/78
5750003	SBE834T	405269	Louth	Louth-Goulceby	8/78	7/82
			Barnsley	crewbus		by 12/85
5750004	MFS342P	405356	Lockerbie	Lockerbie-Waterbeck	11/75	4/78
			Falkirk	reserve		8/80
5750005	KCD512P	405362	Newbury	reserve	8/75	8/81
			Maidstone	crewbus		6/82
5750006	PCW970T	405365	Ulverston	Ulverston-Grizedale Forest	6/79	9/82
5750007	UFO273S	405414	Llandrindod Wells	reserve	6/78	3/83
5750008	OCY702R	405479	Llandovery	Llandovery-Myddfai	7/77	8/81
5750009	MWV807P	405458	Chichester	Regional Reserve	7/76	10/82
			Maidstone	crewbus		
5750010	VAP158S	405438	Canterbury	Canterbury-Crundale	1/78	2/83
5750011	RTX183R	405499	Llandovery	Regional reserve	7/77	
			Rhyl	reserve	10/77	
			Builth Wells	Builth Wells-Abergwesyn	11/79	
			Rhyl	reserve	5/80	2/84
5750012	NWM606S	405516	Liverpool-71	crewbus	10/77	4/84
5750013	RTT378R	405533	Honiton	Honiton-Luppitt	11/76	12/76
			Wadebridge	Wadebridge-Penrose	9/77	2/81
5750014	NWM605S	405378	Liverpool-75	crewbus	10/77	12/83
5750015	LYJ353P	405560	Henley-on-Thames	Henley-Frieth	9/76	7/82
5750016	MFS343P	405566	Aberfoyle	Aberfoyle-Inversnaid	4/76	7/80
5750017	TNJ701S	405623	Canterbury	Canterbury-Crundale	8/77	
			Canterbury	reserve	1/78	4/85
5750018	NWM604S	405638	Liverpool-79	crewbus	10/77	12/83
5750019	RCJ364R	405652	Rhyl	Rhyl-Meriadog	10/77	8/82
5750020	NSX881P	405918	Newtonmore	Newtonmore-Kinlochlaggan	3/76	7/80
5750021	RMS411P	405922	Callander	Callander-Trossachs	3/76	8/80
5750022	KUF288P	406044	Redhill	crewbus (psv licensed)	2/76	-/77
			Redhill	crewbus		7/81
5750023	NWM603S	405981	Liverpool-91	crewbus	10/77	3/84
5750024	KYO838P	405954	London (Camden)	crewbus	11/75	5/82
5750025	KSM205P	406062	Lockerbie	reserve	3/76	
			Dunoon	reserve	7/78	8/80
5750026	KSB746P	405990	Luing	Isle of Luing	5/76	
			Oban	reserve	8/78	9/80
5750027	LAS415P	406023	Applecross	Applecross-Toscaig	6/76	7/80
5750028	NWM607S	406094	Liverpool-R1	crewbus	10/77	6/84
5750029	KYO844P	406079	London (Camden)	crewbus	10/75	5/82
5750030	OBC529P	406180	Billesdon-R5	reserve	8/76	
			Billesdon	Billesdon services	11/78	9/79
5750031	MGE970P	406044	Biggar	Biggar-Newbigging	8/76	6/80
5750032	KJS4R	405288	Timsgarry	Timsgarry-Callanish/Stornoway	4/77	10/80
5750033	LGP120P	406182	Croydon	crewbus	11/75	5/82
5750034	PRP761R	406215	Milton Keynes	crewbus	8/76	9/82
5750035	LSW817R	406241	Kirkcudbright	Kirkcudbright-Borgue	10/76	9/80
5750036	TFS326R	406266	Kinross	Kinross-Rumbling Bridge	2/77	10/80
5750037	LYK751P	406275	London (Camden)	crewbus	4/76	5/82
5750038	TWO958S	406233	Usk	Usk-Llandenny	7/78	5/82
5750039	RUS790R	406261	Ardgay	Ardgay-Strathoykel	12/76	
			Aberfeldy	Aberfeldy-Lawers	8/78	10/80
			Edinburgh-PE22	crewbus		4/82
5750040	MSB699R	405948	Lochboisdale	reserve	12/76	9/80
5750041	TWO957S	406284	Usk	Usk-Bettws Newydd	7/78	
			Llanidloes	reserve	8/81	
			Newtown	reserve	c9/81	4/83
5750042	TFO140S	406318	Llandrindod Wells	Llandrindod Wells-Llaithddu	6/78	2/83
5750043	WMS147R	406297	Lochinver	Lochinver-Drumbeg	12/76	
			Lochboisdale	reserve	1/79	
			Lochmaddy	Lochmaddy-Sidinish	9/79	12/80
5750044	USG706R	406380	Elgol	Elgol-Broadford	12/76	12/80
5750045	USG705R	406359	Castlebay	Castlebay-Eoligarry	4/77	12/80
5750046	XUF880T	410016	Dorking	Dorking-Ockley	9/78	9/84
5750047	USG707R	410048	Lochmaddy	Lochmaddy-Benbecula	4/77	12/80
5750048	USG708R	410076	Strathconon	Strathconon-Muir of Ord-Tomich	1/77	12/80
5750049	USG709R	410087	Skerray	Skerray-Tongue	2/77	10/80
5750050	AJU571T	410131	Billesdon	Billesdon services	11/78	9/79
			Abergavenny	reserve	2/80	5/83

5750051	XMS40R	410146	Crianlarich	Crianlarich-Callander	5/77	11/80
			Glenrothes	crewbus	by 5/81	6/82
5750052	UFS864R	410117	Alligin	Alligin-Kinlochewe	2/77	10/80
5750053	XUF890T	410254	Oxted	Oxted-Lingfield	9/78	
			Chichester	driver-trainer	7/84	7/85
5750054	UFS865R	410260	Islay	Islay services	1/77	
			West Calder	West Calder-Tarbrax	4/79	1/81
5750055	RUS797R	410291	Abington	Abington-Crawfordjohn	3/77	
			Biggar	reserve	5/78	2/81
5750056	UFS866R	410203	Biggar	Biggar-Tweedsmuir	1/77	2/81
5750057	ANJ554T	410223	Sittingbourne	Sittingbourne-Wormshill	1/79	8/84
5750058	NSB234R	410240	Oban	reserve	2/77	12/80
5750059	VSF992R	410207	Cupar	Cupar-Peat Inn	1/77	1/81
5750060	KJS830R	410321	Lochboisdale	written off on delivery 2/77	-	-
5750061	MSM963R	410344	Lockerbie	Lockerbie-St Ann's/Hightae	1/77	2/81
5750062	NAS2R	410340	Scourie	Scourie-Kylestrome	3/77	1/81
5750063	NAS3R	410305	Lairg	reserve	3/77	1/81
5750064	NSB334R	410369	Islay	Islay services	3/77	
			Stornoway	reserve	5/79	12/80
5750065	NSB335R	410392	Port Ellen	reserve	3/77	
			Islay	Islay services	-/79	1/81
5750066	MSM964R	410454	Castle Douglas	reserve	3/77	12/80
5750067	NSB336R	410482	Islay	Islay services	3/77	1/81
5750068	MSM965R	410437	Thornhill	Thornhill-Moniaive	3/77	2/81
			Darlington	postal engineering	-/81	2/82
5750069	NAS176R	410671	Dingwall	reserve	3/77	2/81
5750070	KJS962R	410653	Castlebay	Castlebay-Eoligarry	4/77	3/81
5750071	NSB492R	410737	Inveraray	Inveraray-Dalmally	5/77	12/80
5750072	NSB493R	410758	Brodick	Brodick-Shannochie	8/77	1/81
5750073	MSW939R	410687	Tigharry	Tigharry-Benbecula	4/77	3/81
5750074	RSD355R	410758	Brodick	Brodick-Pirnmill	8/77	1/81
5750075	HMS663S	410803	Denny	Denny-Fintry	3/78	4/81
5750076	CFS720S	410691	West Calder	West Calder-Tarbrax	2/78	12/78
			Linlithgow	Linlithgow-Blackness	1/79	4/81
			Edinburgh PE21	postal engineering	by10/81	7/82
5750077	BFS632S	410868	Kirriemuir	Kirriemuir-Glen Clova	6/78	2/81
5750078♦	USL606S	410904	Blairgowrie	Blairgowrie-Glenshee	4/78	11/81
			Glasgow	postal engineering		8/82
5750079	YGD387S	411037	Strathaven	Strathaven-Dungavel	4/78	3/82
5750080	GSG94T	411084	Gorebridge	Gorebridge-Moorfoot	3/79	2/82
			Perth-47	crewbus	c5/82	
5750081	KHR874P	10451	Swindon	crewbus	10/75	9/84
5750082	LLJ691P	10452	Southampton	crewbus	10/75	6/83
5750083	LFS954P	934030M	Durness	Durness-Rispond	9/75	
			Lochinver	Lochinver-Drumbeg	1/79	4/80
5750084	LFS951P	933175M	Poolewe	Poolewe-Cove	9/75	4/80
5750085	LFS953P	933870M	Lairg	Lairg-Altass	9/75	4/80
5750086	LFS952P	933267M	Plockton	Plockton-Stromeferry	9/75	-/79
5750087	LFS960P	935807M	Melvich	Melvich-Forsinard	11/75	5/80

RSD354R (5750105) was one of the ten Land Rovers converted from mailvans to postbuses. It inaugurated the Brodick-Kilmory route in January 1978 but is here pictured substituting on the Brodick to Black- waterfoot service.
Photobus Eckersley

29

5750088	LFS959P	935806M	Locheport	Locheport-Sidinish	10/75	
			Grimsay	Grimsay-Carinish	4/77	
			Castlebay	reserve	4/79	-/80
5750089	LFS958P	935801M	Grimsay	Grimsay-Carinish	10/75	
			Locheport	Locheport-Sidinish	4/77	
			Dunvegan	reserve	4/79	6/80
5750090	MFS332P	936024M	Kirriemuir	Kirriemuir-Glen Prosen	1/76	4/80
5750091	MFS333P	936112M	Balfron	Balfron-Fintry	2/76	6/80
5750092	NSX876P	934587M	Forres	Forres-Braemoray	1/76	6/80
5750093	NSX878P	935291M	Lockerbie	Lockerbie-Corrie Common	1/76	5/80
5750094	OSC504P	935849M	Lairg	reserve	3/76	6/80
5750095	NSX879P	935799M	Bernera	Bernera-Callanish	4/77	6/80
5750096	OSC505P	936047M	Craignure	Craignure-Lochbuie	4/76	1/81
5750097	OSC507P	936039M	West Linton	West Linton-Romanno Bridge	9/76	6/80
5750098	MFS335P	90611249A	Arnisdale	Arnisdale-Glenelg	10/75	7/81
5750099	MFS345P	90611250A	Invergarry	Invergarry-Kinlochourn	2/76	12/81
5750100	MFS336P	90611251A	Dalwhinnie	Dalwhinnie-Drummin	11/75	8/81
			Dunfermline	workshop van	by 5/82	
5750101	NSX877P	90611255A	Colonsay	Isle of Colonsay	2/76	1/83
5750102	OSC506P	90611256A	Thurso	reserve	1/76	10/81
5750103	JSK111P	90611257A	Halkirk	Halkirk-Altnabreac	9/76	10/81
5750104	OSN830R	90611263A	Pitlochry	Pitlochry-Dalnaspidal	11/76	3/78
			Ballater	Ballater-Linn of Dee	3/78	10/81
5750105	RSD354R	90611264A	Brodick	Brodick-Kilmory	1/78	
			Brodick	reserve	9/81	4/83
			Dundee	workshop vehicle		
5750106	KSA948P	90611203A	Huntly	mailvan	10/75	
			Hawick	Hawick-Craik	11/76	4/77
			Brodick	Brodick-Blackwaterfoot	8/77	1/80
5750107	KSA947P	90611214A	Huntly	mailvan	10/75	
			Invergordon	Invergordon-Kildermorie	10/76	4/77
			Stornoway	reserve	4/77	
			Perth	reserve	5/79	11/81
			Perth-P85	postal engineering	11/81	
			Perth	workshop van	by 7/86	
5750108	KSA950P	90611253A	Aboyne	mailvan	-/75	
			Aberfeldy	Aberfeldy-Birnam	10/76	3/78
			Pitlochry	dual-purpose reserve		4/84
5760001	LAC906P	BCLBRK64846	Rugby	Postal Training College	7/75	8/82

The 1985 Postbus purchases were largely Commer 11-seaters, but also included two Sherpa buses, fifteen Marina estates and eleven Land Rovers. Delivered as 5750099, MFS345P later became 5770099, and was allocated throughout its working life to the Invergarry-Kinlochourn route.
Photobus Eckersley

1976

1976 failed to sustain the growth in services enjoyed the previous year and no further 11-seaters were bought as many earlier Commers were still standing at workshops awaiting allocation. Three of the year's delivery of fifty Land Rover vans were converted at Inverness into dual-purpose postbus/mailvan reserves, 6100042 also carrying a yellow beacon for use as a workshop vehicle.

6100001-6100050   Land Rover 88" 60cf. mailvan (*4-seat dual-purpose postbus)

serial	registration	chassis no.	location	route	in	out
6100041*	PAS537S	90616775A	Inverness	dual-purpose reserve	by 7/78	
6100042*	NAS432R	90616776A	Kyle of Lochalsh	dual-purpose reserve	4/77	10/86
6100047*	PAS536S	90616799A	Inverness	dual-purpose reserve	12/77	6/86

One of the three 1976 Land Rover mailvans converted to dual-purpose reserves was NAS432R (6100042), based at Kyle of Lochalsh. It is photographed substituting for the regular Land Rover on the Arnisdale to Kyle of Lochalsh service. *P Walton*

1977

1977 saw an increase in the use of estate cars on lightly loaded routes in Scotland and orders changed to the Chrysler Avenger with thirty-two in three batches - five purchased locally in Scotland, the main batch of twenty-six, and a single vehicle from Cannon of Coatbridge to replace accident victim 4750034 on the Kylesku to Elphin service. Avenger 7750002 was destroyed when hit by another vehicle while parked outside the Post Office at Rhynie in December 1977, and with no suitable replacement the Huntly to Lumsden route was suspended until replacement 7750010 entered service the following March. 7750001/3-32 were renumbered 7760001/3-32 in 1980.

The Commer range had received a facelift, the main external difference being the addition of a black and silver plastic grille, and had been relaunched as the Dodge Spacevan. Twenty of the new design but still with Rootes PSV conversion were delivered in June to October 1978 to replace earlier vehicles and to commence new services. 7750049 was allocated to the Rothbury to Biddlestone service but was damaged during driver-training and so the intended reserve took over. 7750044/9 became 7780044/9 in 1980.

7750001-7750032	Chrysler Avenger 4-seat estate car postbus
7750033-7750052	Dodge 2000LB 11-seat Postbus (Rootes conversion)

The Chrysler Avenger estate car was favoured for estate car postbuses in 1977 with a large purchase of thirty-two including OSM672S (7750009) photographed at its Lockerbie base in September 1979. *P. Walton*

serial	registration	chassis no.	location	route	in	out
7750001	UFS867R	127076	Invergordon	Invergordon-Kildermorie	4/77	5/81
7750002	UFS868R	127077	Huntly	Huntly-Lumsden	5/77	12/77
7750003	UFS869R	127078	Kelso	Kelso-Smailholm	4/77	4/81
			Glasgow	postal engineering		7/82
7750004	UFS870R	127079	Dollar	Dollar-Glendevon	5/77	4/81
7750005	UFS871R	127081	Hawick	Hawick-Craik	4/77	5/81
			Glasgow	workshop supervisor's car		8/83
7750006	FSC812S	113450	Anstruther	Anstruther-Arncroach	7/78	9/81
7750007	YFS507S	113451	Annan	Annan-Creca	4/78	10/82
7750008	HMS223S	113452	Dunblane	Dunblane-Braco	3/78	7/81
7750009	OSM672S	113453	Lockerbie	Lockerbie-Hightae	4/78	
			Lockerbie	Lockerbie-Waterbeck	4/82	10/82
7750010	VSA322S	113454	Huntly	Huntly-Lumsden	3/78	10/83
7750011	OSM670S	113455	Glenluce	Glenluce-New Luce	2/78	5/83
7750012	OSM673S	113456	Lockerbie	Lockerbie-Waterbeck	4/78	4/82
7750013	LSK631S	113457	Strathy	Strathy-Strathy Point	6/78	5/83
7750014	JPS762S	113458	Bressay	Isle of Bressay	3/78	6/83
7750015	RKS816S	113459	Melrose	Melrose-Maxton	4/78	7/83
7750016	FSC811S	113460	Cupar	Cupar-Birkhill	7/78	2/82
7750017	OST184S	113461	Roy Bridge	Roy Bridge-Moy	3/78	5/84
7750018	RKS213S	113462	Peebles	Peebles-Manorhead	3/78	2/83
7750019	YGD388S	113463	Abington	Abington-Crawfordjohn	5/78	4/82
7750020	RKS214S	113464	Duns	Duns-Abbey St. Bathans	4/78	11/82
7750021	FSC810S	113465	Cupar	Cupar-Brunton	7/78	9/82
7750022	FSC809S	113466	Cupar	Cupar-Newburgh	7/78	11/81
7750023	SST163T	113467	Ardgay	Ardgay-Strathoykel	8/78	8/82
7750024	SST971T	113468	Dunvegan	Dunvegan-Skinidin-Borreraig	11/78	8/81
			Portree	reserve	9/81	
			Kyle	reserve		5/84
7750025	RSB428S	113469	Bridge of Orchy	Bridge of Orchy-Dalmally	3/78	11/82
7750026	JBS251S	113470	Rousay	Isle of Rousay	3/78	6/82
7750027	RKS207S	113471	Kelso	Kelso-Hassington	6/78	3/84
7750028	SST972T	113472	Dunvegan	Dunvegan-Glendale-Borreraig	11/78	6/84
7750029	TSR663S	113473	Aberfeldy	Aberfeldy-Birnam	3/78	4/81
7750030	TSR662S	113474	Pitlochry	Pitlochry-Dalnaspidal	3/78	3/81
7750031	SST973T	113475	Dunvegan	Dunvegan-Waternish	11/78	6/84
7750032	OST608S	144372	Kylesku	Kylesku-Elphin	9/77	4/82
7750033	SSH158T	431859	Galashiels	Galashiels-Lilliesleaf	8/78	4/83
7750034	WSP488T	431907	Aberfeldy	Aberfeldy-Glen Lyon	9/78	11/81
7750035	SSM390T	431898	Castle Douglas	Castle Douglas-Mossdale	8/78	1/83
7750036	SST164T	431983	Nairn	Nairn-Glenferness	8/78	7/82
7750037	GSG 90T	431897	Dunbar	Dunbar-Innerwick	10/78	2/83
7750038	SSH836T	431893	Hawick	Hawick-Bonchester Bridge	11/78	6/82
7750039	TSB341T	431908	Islay	Islay services	9/78	10/82
7750040	TKS16T	431894	Kelso	Kelso-Stichill	11/78	6/83
			Perth-47	crewbus	by 11/83	7/84
7750041	JSC776T	431985	Leven	Leven-New Gilston	10/78	9/82
7750042	TSB771T	432061	Port Ellen	reserve	11/78	8/83
7750043	XVJ231T	431987	Newtown	Newtown-New Mills	6/79	6/83
7750044	DWC836T	432147	Diss	Diss-Gislingham	2/79	11/82
			Harlow	crewbus		
7750045	URN188V	432010	Barrow-in-Furness	reserve	8/78	9/82
7750046	YBB576T	432122	Alnwick	Rothbury-Alwinton	7/79	10/83
7750047	ENJ202V	432096	Redhill	Redhill-Outwood	10/79	3/85
7750048	FAP447V	432133	Henley HTR4	reserve	11/79	c4/84
7750049	VTN164T	432128	Rothbury	reserve	1/79	
			Wakefield	crewbus	4/82	
7750050	VTN165T	432118	Rothbury	Rothbury-Biddlestone	1/79	4/83
7750051	ANJ530T	432152	Tunbridge Wells	Tunbridge Wells-Mayfield	5/79	4/85
7750052	DUF936V	432049	Heathfield	Heathfield-Waldron	8/79	
			Eastbourne	reserve	9/84	
			Redhill	reserve	1/85	8/85

1978

In 1978 Scottish Postal Board purchased five diesel-engined Ford Transits with Dormobile 16-seat bodies, the first to upgrade the busy Isle of Luing service was obtained from Blythswood Motors of Glasgow in plain white and repainted red at Lockerbie. Two of the other four were downseated to replace both the Leyland Boxer and the reserve Terrier on the Laide-Achnasheen service which had proved so expensive to run that Highland Regional Council had made good a loss of £1,898 the previous year. Nine more petrol-engined Dodges with Rootes conversions were ordered for Wales, however four were diverted elsewhere to fulfil more pressing duties, and 8750003 was sent to Kendal for a service which failed to materialise. Four Dodge crewbuses with low roof, longitudinal seating and Perkins diesel engines were delivered for staff transport; they were renumbered 8780015-8 in 1980 and 8750003/6 later became 8780003/6 when used as crewbuses. Four Land Rover 88" 60cf mailvans out of forty were converted to Postbuses at Lockerbie in September 1979 before entering service, 8100016/34/34/36 becoming 8750019-22 in order and later further renumbered 8770019-22 in the 1980 renumbering.

Land Rover postbus MSE408V (8150021) is seen in the yard of Grantown-on-Spey Post Office awaiting its next trip to Lochindorb. The rear step, white roof and King's cypher features are visible in this view.
M W Skillen

serial	registration	chassis no.	location	route	in	out
8750001	HSC 830T	BDVPUJ33168	Luing	Isle of Luing	9/78	5/84
8750002	CDW 273V	613891	Abergavenny	Abergavenny-Skenfrith	2/80	2/85
			Abergavenny-R7	reserve		8/87
8750003	WFV 989V	613896	Penrith	reserve	6/80	5/83
			Liverpool	crewbus	by 6/84	
8750004	WEJ 213V	613890	Aberystwyth	Aberystwyth-Blaenpennal	1/80	4/83
8750005	GCD 279V	613892	Petworth	Petworth-Bignor	2/80	3/85
8750006	LAR 790V	613894	Diss	reserve	3/80	11/82
			Harlow	crewbus		
8750007	CFO 347V	613897	Builth Wells	Builth Wells-Abergwesyn	5/80	4/83
			Llandrindod Wells	reserve		1/84
8750008	CFO 348V	613893	Llandrindod Wells	Llandrindod Wells-Rhayader	5/80	5/83
			Llandrindod Wells	reserve		4/84
8750009	DCJ 73V	613895	Llanidloes	Llanidloes-Llangurig	7/80	7/85
8750010	WFV 985V	613898	Broughton in Furness	Broughton-Cockley Beck	2/80	9/82
8750011	TST 965T	BDVPUR253479	Laide	Laide-Achnasheen	4/79	2/84
8750012	TST 966T	BDVPWC420610	Dingwall	reserve (for Laide)	4/79	2/84
8750013	VLS 861T	BDVPWC420620	Killin	Killin-Callander	4/79	4/84
8750014	ESU 513T	BDVP??413190	Dunoon	Dunoon-Tighnabruaich	5/79	1/84
8750015	UWM 133V	AD620000	Liverpool	crewbus	2/80	
8750016	BOP 693V	AD620001	Birmingham	crewbus	2/80	
8750017	VTK 322V	AD620002	Plymouth-41	crewbus	2/80	
8750018	FUU 679V	AD620003	London (Camden)	crewbus	4/80	
8750019	DSD 319V	90626944A	Brodick	Brodick-Blackwaterfoot	1/80	6/84
			Glasgow	workshop van	by 9/87	
8750020	VST 489V	90627190A	Killilan	Killilan-Dornie	2/80	5/84
8750021	MSE 408V	90627193A	Grantown-on-Spey	Grantown-Lochindorb	6/80	5/85
			Berneray	mailvan	6/85	
8750022	YAS 14V	90627208A	Tomatin	Tomatin-Coignafearn	8/80	1/85

Header reference (vehicle types):

8750001	Ford Transit with Dormobile B16F bodywork
8750002-8750010	Dodge PBCM2090L 11-seat Postbus (Rootes conversion)
8750011-8750014	Ford Transit with Dormobile B16F bodywork (*B12F plus mail)
8750015-8750018	Dodge 2090P 12-seat personnel carrier
8750019-8750022	Land Rover 88" 4-seat Postbus

The route from Diss to Gislingham was unusual in serving Suffolk villages although starting and finishing just over the border in Norfolk. It ran for eleven years from March 1974, being withdrawn at short notice in June 1985 after its subsidies were cut by Suffolk CC. Pictured with Dodge LAR790V (8750006) is of the eight regular drivers.
Photobus

1979

In 1979, by contrast to the small number of new services, a large delivery of Postbuses took place, including another sixteen Avenger estate cars delivered in the summer, the first entering service in November, 9750009/16 replacing dual-purpose Land Rovers. 9750010 was delivered new to Bamber Bridge in July 1979, and moved to Chester suggesting it was ordered for a new route in North West which failed to materialise; eventually it was sent to Milton Keynes as an ordinary car. The Avengers had a mixture of Chrysler (confirmed for 9750002/3/4/5/6/7/11/5/6) or Talbot (9750008/14) badging, and all sixteen were renumbered 9760001-9760009, 9720128, 9760011-9760016 in 1980.

The biggest order of the year was for eighty-six Dodges with Rootes conversion, and again entry to service was protracted with many kept in pools for long periods. Examples of this batch remained at Lockerbie after the following year's order were all in service and the last few were released at the end of 1983 to replace earlier vehicles of the same batch. However the last to enter service is also the most famous being 9750066 that was sent to Lockerbie pool, then Chester pool in May 1983 with the intention of it becoming a regional reserve for Wales before moving to Dorking where it finally entered service on 28th August 1984. It worked the Ockley route for less than a year, being demoted to a driver trainer and then crewbus before being bought by David Cott for preservation. 9750030 was initially allocated to Penrith for an intended service at Kirkby Stephen. 9750057 was never used by the Post Office and after storage at Maidstone and then Lockerbie, it moved to Kidbrooke for registration prior to donation to Stockwell Park Estate Community with only 819 miles on the clock. Several were used as crewbuses, some from new (9750023 being renumbered 9780023 before registration), and 9750028/9/30/46/80/5 were later renumbered 9780028/9/30/46/80/5 to reflect their changed status.

Further Ford Transits with Dormobile bodywork for use in Scotland included one more purpose-built minibus and four short wheel-base panel vans converted by Dormobile (at least one of which was delivered in white and repainted at Lockerbie), bought locally as a pair and two singles because of the delays in delivery of the Dodges. 9750103 was upseated to B14F by August 1981.

Four of the order for forty-eight Land Rovers were converted to 4-seaters, at least one of which was carried out at Thurso workshop. Two (9100019/25) retained their mailvan serials but the other two (9100027/31) were renumbered into the Land Rover postbus series by changing the second and third digits to become 9770027/31.

Opposite, top:- **The final five vehicles of the 1979 Postbus order were Ford Transits. One was a 16-seater, with the last four having 11-seats. Of those, two became Reserves, including EMS 953V (9750105) seen here working the Crianlarich route.** *Photobus Eckersley*
Opposite, bottom:- **The Post Office has owned a number of larger buses, PDU 355W (9760001, later 9780001) being allocated to Coton House Postal Management College. The Bedford VAS model with Plaxton bodywork is seen visiting Reading MLO in June 1989.** *D A Cott*

The Postbus Handbook

The final 1979 purchase was 9760001, a Bedford VAS5 with Plaxton Supreme C29F bodywork as a non-psv for the Rugby College, by then known as Coton House Management College. It was renumbered 9780001 (possibly before entry to service), and was finished in a cream livery with a broad orange waistband.

9100001-9100048	Land Rover 88" 60cf. mailvan (* converted to 4-seat postbus)
9750001-9750016	Chrysler/Talbot Avenger 1600 4-seat estate car postbus
9750017-9750102	Dodge 2090P 11-seat postbus (Rootes conversion)
9750103	Ford Transit with Dormobile B10F bodywork
9750104-9750107	Ford Transit 11-seat postbus (Dormobile conversion)
9760001	Bedford VAS5 with Plaxton Supreme C29F coachwork

serial	registration	chassis no.	location	route	in	out
9100019*	AAS837W	112307	Lairg	dual-purpose reserve	8/80	8/90
9100025*	DAS877W	112808	Dingwall (later R3)	dual-purpose reserve	7/81	
9100027*	VSA242X	112972	Huntly	reserve	5/82	
			Huntly	dual-purpose reserve	c7/86	5/87
9100031*	PSK373W	113934	Bettyhill	Bettyhill-Kinbrace	1/81	8/84
9750001	SSF175V	173544	Kinross	Kinross-Cleish	1/80	1/84
9750002	KBS594V	173545	Sanday	Lady-Sanday	1/80	6/84
9750003	KBS595V	173546	Sanday	Isle of Sanday	1/80	6/84
9750004	XSB547V	173547	Tarbert	Tarbert-Skipness	5/80	5/84
9750005	XKS371V	173548	Selkirk	Selkirk-Ashkirk	4/80	5/84
9750006	VST484V	173549	Kyle of Lochalsh	Plockton-Stromeferry	1/80	8/84
9750007	BSN667V	173550	Kirriemuir	Glen Prosen	4/80	5/84
9750008	XKS348V	173551	Kelso	Kelso-Roxburgh	5/80	6/84
9750009	XKS372V	173552	Galashiels	reserve	4/80	5/84
9750010	WEV68W	173553	Milton Keynes	Technical Training College (crewbus)	6/81	
9750011	VFF558V	173554	Machynlleth	Machynlleth-Aberhosan	12/79	1/85
9750012	XST234V	212640	Poolewe	Poolewe-Cove	4/80	5/84
9750013	PSK266W	212639	Skerray	Skerray-Tongue	10/80	6/84
9750014	AST686W	212638	Dingwall	Dingwall-Heights of Dochcarty	12/80	6/84
9750015	VSM785V	180076	Lockerbie	Lockerbie-Corrie Common	5/80	5/84
9750016	ASM157W	180075	Lockerbie	reserve	11/79	6/84
9750017	ESL559V	AD619849	Pitlochry	reserve	6/80	6/85
9750018	USC643V	AD619850	Haddington	Haddington-Garvald	6/80	10/83
9750019	VSF335V	AD619851	Cupar	reserve	4/80	3/86
9750020	MLS117W	AD619852	Falkirk	reserve	8/80	12/85
9750021	VSM787V	AD619853	Castle Douglas	Castle Douglas-Auchencairn	6/80	1/84
9750022	NGD817V	AD619854	Biggar	Biggar-Newbigging	6/80	1/84
9780023	NVM284W	AD619855	Manchester	Regional PRO (crewbus)	by 1/81	
9750024	CNL365V	AD619856	Chathill	Chathill-Bamburgh	5/80	3/85
9750025	CNL366V	AD619857	Alnwick-R5	reserve	6/80	1/86
9750026	CVK52V	AD619858	Morpeth	reserve	7/80	1/86
9750027	JTT871V	AD619859	Honiton	Honiton-Luppitt	7/80	7/85
9750028	MBU814V	AD619860	Oldham-43	crewbus		
			Blackburn-25	crewbus	5/81	by 2/82
9750029	WRN22Y	AD619861	Ulverston	Ulverston-Grizedale Forest	9/82	10/84
			Barrow-in-Furness	reserve	10/84	
			Liverpool	crewbus		
			North West	postal engineering	by 3/86	
9750030	GAO301V	AD619862	Penrith	Penrith-Martindale	5/80	5/83
			Liverpool	crewbus	5/83	
9750031	DCW328W	AD619863	Kirkby Stephen	(proposed route)	4/80	
			Barrow-in-Furness	reserve	11/80	6/85
			Ulverston	Ulverston-Grizedale Forest	10/84	5/85
9750032	WRN23Y	AD619864	Barrow-in-Furness	reserve	9/82	10/84
			Ulverston	Ulverston-Grizedale Forest	10/84	5/85
9750033	WRN24Y	AD619865	Broughton-in-Furness	Broughton-Cockley Beck	9/82	6/85
9750034	YAS371V	AD619866	Applecross	Applecross-Toscaig	7/80	12/82
			Dingwall	reserve		1/83
			Lairg	reserve	by 6/83	by 3/84
9750035	XST986V	AD619867	Dingwall	Dingwall-Heights of Dochcarty	6/80	12/80
			Clarkston	Clarkston-Carmunnock	4/82	4/85
9750036	SGA22W	AD619868	Dunoon	reserve	10/80	12/80
			Galashiels	reserve	12/80	6/85

9750037	XAS109V	AD619869	Kyle of Lochalsh	reserve	8/80	5/85
9750038	JRS937V	AD619870	Aboyne	Aboyne-Logie Coldstone	8/80	2/84
9750039	KLS132V	AD619871	Aberfoyle	Aberfoyle-Inversnaid	7/80	2/84
9750040	XSM314V	AD619872	Lockerbie	reserve	7/80	3/85
9750041	HFG552V	AD619873	Redhill	reserve	7/80	
			Oxted	Oxted-Lingfield	7/84	3/85
9750042	JAP606V	AD619874	Hungerford	Hungerford-Lambourn	6/80	
			Newbury	Regional Reserve	8/81	8/85
9750043	ASB327W	AD619875	Oban	reserve	9/80	5/85
9750044	AST136W	AD619876	Alligin	Alligin-Kinlochewe	10/80	4/85
9750045	YST509W	AD619877	Elgol	Elgol-Broadford	12/80	3/85
9750046	RTW483W	AD619878	Milton Keynes	Technical Training College	5/81	
9750047	XSW486W	AD619879	Kirkcudbright	Kirkcudbright-Borgue	9/80	2/84
9750048	XSM315V	AD619880	Annan	Annan-Powfoot	7/80	4/85
9750049	XSM316V	AD619881	Castle Douglas	Castle Douglas-Corsock	7/80	11/84
9750050	YSG781W	AD619882	Kinross-K7	Kinross-Rumbling Bridge	10/80	5/85
9750051	UJS503W	AD619883	Castlebay	Castlebay-Eoligarry	12/80	3/86
9750052	FSR861W	AD619884	Aberfeldy	Aberfeldy-Lawers	10/80	2/84
9750053	XAS110V	AD619885	Newtonmore	Newtonmore-Kinlochlaggan	7/80	2/84
9750054	UJS117W	AD619886	Timsgarry	Timsgarry-Callanish/Stornoway	10/80	5/83
9750055	LMS985W	AD619887	Callander	Callander-Trossachs	8/80	4/85
9750056	JSJ716W	AD619888	Brodick	Brodick-Pirnmill	1/81	2/84
			Port Ellen	reserve	3/84	5/85
9750057	PGJ838Y	AD619889	Lockerbie workshop	awaiting allocation	not used	6/83
9750058	A994HSM	AD619890	Castle Douglas	Castle Douglas-Auchencairn	1/84	8/86
			Oldham-8	crewbus		by 6/88
9750059	A680RNS	AD619891	Biggar-M53	Biggar-Newbiggins	1/84	7/87
9750060	OSC695Y	AD619892	Dunbar	Dunbar-Innerwick	2/83	c2/84
9750061	BSC389W	AD619893	West Calder	West Calder-Tarbrax	1/81	4/85
9750062	FSB254Y	AD619894	Port Askaig	Islay reserve	10/82	3/86
9750063	XSW490W	AD619895	Lockerbie	Lockerbie-St. Ann's	2/81	6/85
9750064	HAS544X	AD619896	Nairn	Nairn-Glenferness	7/82	5/85
9750065	SHS867W	AD619897	Biggar	Biggar-Tweedsmuir	2/81	4/85
9750066	B449GUF	AD619898	Dorking	Dorking-Ockley	9/84	5/85
			Chichester	driver-trainer	8/85	
			Reading-PC2	crewbus	c2/88	
			Maidenhead	crewbus	1/89	8/89
9750067	XSW491W	AD619899	Thornhill	Thornhill-Moniaive	1/81	7/85
9750068	BST789W	AD619900	Dingwall	reserve	2/81	2/86
9750069	PSC918Y	AD619901	Leven	Leven-New Gilston	9/82	3/86
9750070	CAS467W	AD619902	Castlebay	Castlebay-Eoligarry	3/81	
			Lochboisdale	reserve	by 7/85	11/85
9750071	CAS889W	AD619903	Tigharry	Tigharry-Benbecula	3/81	10/85
9750072	A592DSS	AD619904	Aboyne	Aboyne-Logie Coldstone	2/84	6/85
			Luing	Isle of Luing	9/85	9/88
			Liverpool-C51	crewbus		c1/89
9750073	A496WSD	AD619905	Brodick	Brodick-Pirnmill	2/84	
			Forfar-F4R	reserve	11/85	
9750074	BSH897X	AD619906	Hawick	Hawick-Bonchester Bridge	6/82	2/86
9750075	FSL36W	AD619907	Kirriemuir	Kirriemuir-Glen Clova	2/81	c4/82
			Forfar-R4	reserve	c4/82	12/87

One of the five Dormobile-bodied Ford Transits bought in 1978 was TST966T (8750012) photographed at Achnasheen station covering the Poolewe to Cove service in July 1979.
D J Foster

The sixteen Avenger 1600 estate cars bought in 1979 had a mixture of Chrysler and Talbot badges. This one, VFF558V (9750011), was marked Chrysler and carried a large bilingual sign on the roof proclaiming its rôle as a postbus on the Machynlleth to Aberhosan service. *Photobus Eckersley*

9750076	XSC822W	AD619908	Haddington	reserve	1/81	
			Dunbar	Dunbar-Innerwick	c2/84	5/85
9750077	RTH682Y	AD619909	Newtown-N24	Newtown-New Mills	4/83	12/87
9750078	LYJ621W	AD619910	Chichester	driver-trainer	6/81	
			Redhill	Regional Reserve	7/84	by 5/86
			Sevenoaks 142 to 138	crewbus		-/87
9750079	LPN382W	AD619911	Newbury-NE28	reserve	11/80	
			Wokingham	crewbus	5/86	
9750080	VFG290Y	AD619912	Redhill-61	crewbus	9/82	
			Sittingbourne	Sittingbourne-Wormshill	8/84	4/85
			Chatham-260	crewbus		by 11/89
9750081	MYN553X	AD619913	London (ECDO).	crewbus	4/82	
9750082	LYJ626W	AD619914	Newport, Isle of Wight	reserve	6/81	
			Sandown	crewbus	6/86	
9750083	A61YCU	AD619915	Alnwick	Alnwick-Alnham	10/83	
			Morpeth	reserve	1/86	10/87
9750084	FKS153Y	AD619916	Kelso	Kelso-Stitchill	6/83	3/86
9780085	LTC455Y	AD619917	Bristol	crewbus	2/83	
			Southampton-72	crewbus	6/83	
9750086	HSB189Y	AD619918	Port Ellen	reserve	8/83	3/86
9750087	A314STS	AD619919	Aberfeldy-PY5	Aberfeldy-Lawers	2/84	3/92
9750088	A995HSM	BD619920	Kirkcudbright	Kirkcudbright-Borgue	2/84	7/87
9750089	A285UGA	BD619921	Aberfoyle	Aberfoyle-Inversnaid	2/84	1/88
9750090	A512OAS	BD619922	Newtonmore	Newtonmore-Kinlochlaggan	2/84	5/85
			Falkirk	driver-trainer	by 4/86	
			Lochboisdale	reserve (on Barra)	8/86	c11/88
9750091	LYJ627W	AD619923	Hailsham	reserve	5/81	
			Tunbridge Wells	Regional Reserve	3/84	
			Redhill	reserve	1/85	9/86

Originally allocated to the Kirriemuir-Glen Clova route, Dodge FSL36W (9750075) became a reserve vehicle based at Forfar. As one of the sponsors of *Scottish Opera Go Round*, the Post Office sponsored Scottish Opera with the bus and a large mailvan plus the offer of other facilities. *P Walton*

9750092	CGT907X	BD619924	London (SWDO).	crewbus	10/81	
			Croydon	crewbus	4/82	
9750093	PWY21W	BD619925	Leeds	Regional PRO	by 8/81	
			Wakefield	crewbus		c2/82
			Berwick-on-Tweed	reserve		
			Rothbury	Rothbury-Alwinton	c4/82	7/85
9750094	REP628Y	BD619926	Llandrindod Wells L1	Llandrindod Wells-Rhayader	4/83	10/87
9750095	KTH827X	AD619927	Aberystwyth	Aberystwyth-Blaenpennal	4/83	9/87
9750096	REP629Y	BD619928	Builth Wells	Builth Wells-Abergwesyn	4/83	10/87
			Llandrindod Wells L1	Llandrindod Wells-Rhayader	10/87	11/88
9750097	REP630Y	BD619929	Llandrindod Wells	Llandrindod Wells-Llaithddu	3/83	10/87
9750098	KCY947X	BD619930	Newtown N28-N25	reserve	8/81	6/89
9750099	KCA6Y	BD619931	Rhyl	Rhyl-Meriadog	9/82	8/84
			Builth Wells	Builth Wells-Painscastle	11/84	1/88
9750100	SKG558Y	BD619932	Abergavenny	reserve	5/83	
			Abergavenny	Abergavenny-Skenfrith	2/85	9/87
			Cardiff	crewbus	3/88	
9750101	MTX909X	BD619933	Usk	Usk-Llandenny	5/82	1/85
9750102	VFG297Y	BD619934	Chichester	reserve	10/82	
			Petersfield	reserve	4/85	
			Alton	reserve	-/86	
			Guildford	crewbus	c10/86	11/88
9750103	WAS796V	BDVPWE322720	Tongue	Talmine-Lairg	11/79	6/84
9750104	EMS511V	300820	Aberfoyle	Aberfoyle-Kinlochard	1/80	4/85
9750105	EMS953V	304460	Falkirk	reserve	4/80	2/86
9750106	WSB925V	304500	Tiree	Isle of Tiree	4/80	5/85
9750107	WSH654V	353580	Galashiels	reserve	3/80	
			Dunoon	reserve	12/80	2/86
9760001	PDU355W	KW454617	Rugby	Coton House Management College	11/80	10/89

1980

In November 1980, postbus type code 75 was split to show the type of vehicle, minibuses and larger PSVs taking 75, estate car buses becoming 76, Land Rover buses type code 77 and non-PSVs of all sizes type code 78, the existing fleet being re-coded to suit. Code 76 had previously denoted large passenger vehicles (renumbered to 75 or 78 as appropriate), 77 was fuel tankers and bowser trailers (re-coded to 79) while 78 was previously vacant. The use of crewbuses increased considerably from 1987, initially to transport staff to the large Mechanised Letter Offices and Parcels Concentration Offices being constructed on industrial estates and greenfield sites. Vehicles delivered with type codes other than 75 to 77 are not listed from this point unless they have been used as postbuses at some stage.

Fifteen vehicles from the year's delivery of thirty-eight Land Rover 88" 60cf mailvans were converted to postbuses and another one became a dual-purpose reserve. 0100003/8/10/2/5/6/8/24/5/7, 0100030/2/4/6/7 were re-coded 0770003/8/10/2/5/6/8/24/5/7, 0770030/2/4/6/7 but the dual-purpose reserve retained its mailvan serial 0100038. 0770015 was England's first Land Rover postbus for use at Wooler in bad weather but later moved to Pickering as a mailvan and regained its original serial number. Sister 0770024 covered 2,500 miles each month on the Arnisdale service and clocked up more than 210,000 miles, going through three engines and two gearboxes in its lifetime. 0770027 was originally allocated registration YST515W but delayed entry into service caused it to be voided and re-registered.

Two more batches of Avenger estate cars followed from earlier deliveries in 1980, all with Talbot badges, including GES948W (0760012) photographed at Pitlochry in between runs on the Pitlochry to Dalnaspidal service. *P Walton*

Thirty-six Talbot Avenger estate cars were supplied in two deliveries in spring and summer 1980 although many did not enter service until 1981, being renumbered 07600xx before entry to service. Those already in service in November 1980 had their serials changed from 07500xx to 07600xx. 0760010/11 replaced a further pair of dual-purpose reserve Land Rovers. 0750004/6/18/9/34 were delivered to Llandrindod Wells, presumably for new services in mid-Wales which did not materialise and were used as ordinary cars, 0750018/9/34 were renumbered 0720023/4/34 before entering service and 0750004/6 became 0720022 and 0720036 respectively.

Fifty-four more Dodges, this time converted by Dormobile as sub-contractor to Chrysler, were delivered in the autumn of 1980, but with a general surplus of postbuses many were not immediately required, 0750044 spending almost three years in store at Newport (Gwent), two months at Rhyl and seven months at Chester before entering service at the beginning of 1984. 0750086 was later used as a crewbus and was re-coded 0780086, but others demoted to such duties retained their original serial numbers. The last one in Post Office service, 0750069 ended its days as a crewbus at Canterbury, passing its MoT test at the end of 1989 with little difficulty, and was retained for the Archive Fleet being fully restored at Kidbrooke by June 1993. There were also two pairs of low-roof Dodge crewbuses, 0750001/2 and 0750023/4, which were later renumbered 0780001/2/23/4; the third, 0750023, before entering service.

0100001-0100038	Land Rover 88" 60cf. mailvan (* converted to 4-seat postbus)
0750001-0750002	Dodge 2090P 12-seat personnel carrier
0750003-0750022	Talbot Avenger 1600 4-seat estate car postbus
0750023-0750024	Dodge 2090P 12-seat personnel carrier
0750025-0750040	Talbot Avenger 1600 4-seat estate car postbus
0750041-0750094	Dodge 2090P 11-seat postbus (Dormobile conversion) ‡ 9-seats or † 8-seats

serial	registration	chassis no.	location	route	in	out
0770003*	SSA764X	133468	Ballater	Ballater-Linn o Dee	10/81	5/87
0770008*	CYS381X	133607	Brodick	Brodick-Kilmory	9/81	
			Blairgowrie-P84	Blairgowrie-Glenshee	c11/85	
0770010*	JES995X	133613	Perth	reserve	11/81	
			Blairgowrie	Blairgowrie-Glenshee		
			Falkirk-FK34	workshop vehicle	by 6/85	
			Grangemouth-FK34	workshop vehicle	12/90	
0770012*	SSK163X	133618	Thurso	reserve	10/81	6/87
0770015*	LVK838X	133626	Wooler	reserve	12/81	1/86
			Pickering	mailvan	c7/86	-/87
0770016*	SSK164X	134158	Halkirk	Halkirk-Altnabreac	10/81	6/87
0770018*	EAS234X	134188	Altnaharra	Altnaharra-Rispond	8/81	6/87
0770024*	YST513W	134532	Arnisdale	Arnisdale-Kyle	7/81	6/87
0770025*	EAS235X	134544	Rogart	Rogart-Scibercross	8/81	6/87
0770027*	EAS255X	134580	Dalwhinnie	Dalwhinnie-Drummin	8/81	6/87
0770030*	XGD31W	134622	Gorthleck	Gorthleck-Killen Lodge	7/81	6/87
0770032*	EAS254X	134810	Invergarry	Invergarry-Kinlochourn	12/81	9/86
			Grantown-on-Spey	reserve		6/87
0770034*	VSA246X	134840	Banchory	Banchory-Ballater	8/82	6/87
0770036*	EAS233X	134939	Ardgay	Ardgay-Craigs	8/81	6/87
0770037*	EAS236X	134959	Drumnadrochit	Drumnadrochit-Grotaig	9/81	6/87
0100038*	DAS569W	134979	Grantown-on-Spey	reserve	5/81	
			Kyle of Lochalsh	reserve and workshop van	by 7/86	
0750001	FAM980W	AD620004	Swindon 55 to 73	crewbus	9/80	
0750002	NUR539V	AD620005	Watford	crewbus	6/80	
0750003	SJS964V	214371	Bernera	Bernera-Callanish	6/80	3/81

Typical of the postbuses of the 1970s & 1980s, although the front end was restyled when carrying the Dodge name rather than Commer is LCN631X (0750084). It is seen here in February 1984 after its run from Ripon in Masham, near the Theakston brewery. *D A Cott*

0750004	DHU189V	214372	Bristol	Regional HQ (car)	1/80	11/84
0750005	XST232V	214373	Lochinver	Lochinver-Drumbeg	4/80	6/84
0750006	CNY677V	214374	Cardiff	Regional HQ (car)	2/80	1/84
0760007	PSK445W	214375	Melvich	Melvich-Forsinard	1/81	7/84
0750008	XST233V	214376	Lairg	Lairg-Altass	4/80	6/84
0750009	XKS978V	214377	West Linton	West Linton-Romanno Bridge	6/80	6/84
0760010	FSL37W	214378	Invergarry	Invergarry-Kinlochourn	1/81	
			Pitlochry	reserve	8/81	6/84
0760011	THS470W	214379	Oban	reserve	2/81	5/85
0760012	GES948W	214380	Pitlochry	Pitlochry-Dalnaspidal	3/81	6/85
0750013	ECJ957W	214381	Llandrindod Wells	reserve	9/80	11/81
			Rhayader	Rhayader-Abergwnyu	11/81	2/84
			Llandrindod Wells	reserve	2/84	2/84
			Machynlleth	Machynlleth-Aberhosan	2/84	10/85
0750014	OSK306V	214382	Melvich	Melvich-Forsinard	5/80	1/81
			Anstruther	Anstruther-Arncroach	9/81	5/84
0750015	SJS756V	214383	Lochboisdale	reserve on Barra	5/80	1/86
0750016	MSE449V	214384	Forres	Forres-Braemoray	6/80	5/85
0760017	CAS816W	214385	Applecross	Applecross-Toscaig	3/81	5/85
0720023	NDA214X	214386	Birmingham	Datapost car	4/82	
0720024	NDA215X	214387	Birmingham	Datapost car	4/82	
0750020	XAS106V	214388	Portree-R6	Dunvegan reserve	6/80	
			Aberdeen		10/85	12/85
0750021	PGD73V	214389	Balfron	Balfron-Fintry	6/80	1/85
0750022	XST922V	214390	Lairg	reserve	6/80	5/85
0780023	EAE635W	AD620006	Bath	crewbus	2/81	
0750024	PRO272W	AD620007	Watford-48	crewbus	8/80	
0760025	CAS677W	311436	Bernera	Bernera-Callanish	3/81	6/85
0760026	HSN616W	311437	Aberfeldy	Aberfeldy-Birnam	4/81	6/85
0760027	CST431W	311438	Invergordon	Invergordon-Kildermorie	5/81	5/85

The Postbus Handbook

A number of the 1980 order for Land Rover mailvans were modified and renumbered as postbuses. EAS236X (0770037) was one of a line of Land Rovers allocated to the route which runs both east and west from Drumnadrochit on the northern banks of Loch Ness. Snow can be encountered from October to March as much of the route is over 500 feet above sea level. *Ken Ross collection*

0760028	ASH988W	311439	Kelso	Kelso-Smailholm	4/81	
			Kelso	Kelso-Smailholm/Hassington	6/84	6/85
0760029	VGD439W	311440	Dollar	Dollar-Glendevon	4/81	5/85
0760030	BSG876W	311441	Hawick	Hawick-Craik	5/81	6/85
0760031	WFS79W	311442	Falkirk-RR3	Regional Reserve	5/81	
			Abington	Abington-Crawfordjohn	6/84	11/85
0760032	VYS657W	311443	Dunblane	Dunblane-Braco	7/81	5/85
0760033	JSC645X	311444	Cupar-4	Cupar-Newburgh	11/81	12/85
0720034	MDA580X	311445	Birmingham	Datapost car	11/81	
0760035	KSF5X	313064	Cupar	Cupar-Birkhill	1/82	8/85
0760036	EDS766X	311446	Abington	Abington-Crawfordjohn	4/82	5/84
0760037	GAS604X	311447	Kylesku	Kylesku-Elphin	4/82	12/85
0760038	MSF197X	311448	Falkirk	reserve	4/82	12/85
0760039	PSF739Y	311449	Cupar	Cupar-Brunton	9/82	12/85
0760040	CSM275X	311450	Lockerbie	Lockerbie-Hightae	4/82	12/85
0750041	ETY211W	AD623238	Berwick	crewbus	8/80	
			Wooler	Wooler-Doddington	8/81	2/86
0750042	ETY210W	AD623239	Berwick	crewbus	8/80	
			Wooler	Wooler-Kirknewton	8/81	1/86
0750043	FEV107Y	AD623240	Diss	reserve	11/82	
			Southend-on-Sea	crewbus	6/85	
			Aylesbury	crewbus		
			High Wycombe	crewbus		by 10/87
0750044	A56UTH	AD623241	Llandrindod Wells	reserve	1/84	
			Builth Wells	Builth Wells-Painscastle	6/84	11/84
			Llandrindod Wells	reserve	11/84	6/85
0750045	ECJ958W	AD623242	Llanidloes	Llanidloes-Dylife	9/80	6/85
0750046	AST428W	AD623243	Strathconon	Strathconon-Muir of Ord	12/80	5/85
0750047	AST645W	AD623244	Lochmaddy	Airport	12/80	6/85
			North Uist	(retained)		11/85

0750048	UJS410W	AD623245	Lochboisdale	reserve	9/80	
			Tigharry			6/85
0750049	WFS72W	AD623246	Edinburgh	driver-trainer	9/80	
			Aberdeen	crewbus	7/85	12/85
0750050	UJS504W	AD623247	Lochmaddy	Lochmaddy-Sidinish	12/80	7/85
0750051	TGB791W	AD623248	Inveraray	Inveraray-Dalmally	12/80	3/86
0750052	AFS926W	AD623249	Cupar	Cupar-Peat Inn	1/81	6/85
0750053	FTS881W	AD623250	Crianlarich	Crianlarich-Killin	11/80	2/86
0750054	BST387W	AD623251	Scourie	Scourie-Kylestrome	1/81	5/85
0750055	JSJ717W	AD623252	Brodick	Brodick-Shannochie	1/81	11/83
0750056	GSX426X	AD623253	Gorebridge	Gorebridge-Moorfoot	3/82	3/86
			Oldham-11	crewbus		6/88
0750057	SHS868W	AD623254	Biggar	reserve	2/81	2/86
0750058	TGB793W	AD623255	Port Ellen	Islay services	12/80	3/84
0750059	BST388W	AD623256	Lairg	reserve	1/81	3/86
0750060	XSW492W	AD623257	Castle Douglas	reserve	2/81	7/85
0750061	AST980W	AD623258	Stornoway	reserve	12/80	
			Haddington	reserve	7/84	3/86
0750062	TGB792W	AD623259	Oban	reserve	12/80	4/86
0750063	DSW560Y	AD623260	Castle Douglas	Castle Douglas-Mossdale	1/83	3/86
0750064	KWV635W	AD623261	Hungerford	Hungerford-Kintbury	11/80	-/86
			Chatham-263	crewbus		
0750065	RTW477W	AD623262	Colchester	Colchester-Flatford	11/80	4/81
			Forfar	in store	9/81	
			Kirriemuir	Kirriemuir-Glen Clova	4/82	5/85
0750066	KWV636W	AD623263	Hungerford	Hungerford-Gt Shefford/E Garston	11/80	7/85
0750067	LWV305W	AD623624	Hailsham	Hailsham-Bodle St. Green	2/81	9/84
			Heathfield	Heathfield-Waldron	9/84	12/84
			Eastbourne	reserve	12/84	1/85
			Redhill	reserve	1/85	9/86
0750068	LWV325W	AD623265	Newport, Isle of Wight	Newport-Brighstone	1/81	3/86
			Broadstairs	crewbus		5/86
0750069	WNJ479Y	AD623266	Canterbury-39	Canterbury-Crundale	2/83	4/85
			Canterbury R50 to R146	reserve	4/85	6/91
			Archive Fleet	preserved	by 6/93	current
0750070	LWV326W	AD623267	Newport, Isle of Wight	Newport-Newtown	1/81	3/86
				crewbus		by 12/86
0750071	KWV637W	AD623268	Petersfield	Petersfield-Froxfield	10/80	3/86
0750072	TGB794W	AD623269	Port Ellen	Islay services	12/80	9/85
0750073	A106YSF	AD623270	Haddington	Haddington-Garvald	10/83	
			Haddington	reserve	3/86	12/87
0750074†	SSK861X	AD623271	Thurso	Thurso-Wick Airport	11/82	7/85
0750075‡	JES994X	AD623272	Blairgowrie	Blairgowrie-Glenshee	11/81	6/85
0750076	CFS989W	AD623273	Linlithgow	Linlithgow-Blackness	4/81	3/86
0750077	CGG916W	AD623274	Strathaven	Strathaven-Dungavel	3/82	3/86
0750078	KSN599X	AD623275	Aberfeldy	Aberfeldy-Glenlyon	11/81	3/86
0750079	BJS469Y	AD623276	Timsgarry	Timsgarry-Stornoway	5/83	8/86
0750080	GSH790Y	AD623277	Galashiels	Galashiels-Lilliesleaf	4/83	3/86
0750081	YAO437Y	AD623278	Penrith	Penrith-Martindale	5/83	7/85
0750082	RMS389W	AD623279	Denny	Denny-Fintry	4/81	3/85
0750083	FEV108Y	AD623280	Diss	Diss-Gislingham	11/82	6/95
			Southend-on-Sea	crewbus		
			Harlow	crewbus		by 10/87
0750084	LCN631X	AD623281	Morpeth	driver-trainer	3/81	
			Harrogate	driver-trainer		
			Ripon	Ripon-Masham	3/82	9/87
0750085	LTY113X	AD623282	Morpeth		8/81	
			Louth	Louth-Goulceby	7/82	10/86
0750086	GCU24W	AD623283	Berwick	reserve	11/80	
			Wakefield	crewbus	by 6/83	by 8/88
0750087	LTY112X	AD623284	Rothbury	Rothbury-Biddlestone	4/83	1/86
			Wakefield-29	crewbus		by 12/88
0750088	YAO436Y	AD623307	Penrith	reserve	5/83	7/85
0750089	GGL256W	AD623308	Wadebridge	Wadebridge-Penrose	2/81	9/85
0750090	KTH824X	AD623309	Llandovery-7	Llandovery-Myddfai	8/81	9/87
0750091	ONJ29W	AD623310	Reigate	Reigate-Leigh	7/82	3/85
0750092	RYJ621X	AD623311	Henley-on-Thames HT15	Henley-Frieth	7/82	3/86
			Reading	crewbus at Amersham Road		
			Newbury	crewbus		-/87
0750093	OUF786X	AD623312	Newbury-NE45	Newbury-Brightwalton	8/81	6/86
0750094	OUF787X	AD623313	Newbury-NE46	Newbury-West Ilsley	8/81	6/86

1981

No further 11-seaters were required as many of the previous year's order were still in storage, however fifteen Talbot Avenger estate cars in cherry with black interior trim were delivered in two batches, five in May 1981 and the rest in January 1982. The first spent some time at Kidbrooke before moving to Lockerbie in April 1983 for issue, while the second was diverted to the National TV Licence Records Office at Bristol and renumbered 1720101. 1760002-5 were delivered new to Bristol in May 1981, suggesting their intended use was on estate car postbus routes in the South-West, which evidently came to nothing. 1760013 became the second Avenger to be written off on the Huntly to Lumsden service. Land Rover deliveries consisted of fifteen mailvans ordered as 1100001-15 but renumbered 1100031-45 before registration to avoid clashing with survivors from 1971, and fifteen Land Rover 88" postbuses numbered 1770001-15 delivered in the spring of 1982. The buses did not find immediate use and eight (1770008-14 and 1770002) were renumbered in the mailvan series as 1100050-56/58 before entering service as late as September 1984. 1100053 later reverted to postbus use and regained its original serial 1770011, however sister 1100052 which was delivered to Corby pool in April 1982 and moved to Lockerbie in December that year finally entered service in January 1985 simply re-coded as 1770052. Three other buses (1770004/6/7) became mailvans by re-coding (becoming 1100004/6/7), but surprisingly mailvan 1100045 was converted to a dual-purpose reserve at Aberdeen. The application of whire roofs at Lockerbie ceased in January 1981 with 9750067 and 0750072 being the last two Dodges to be sent out with white roofs and 0750060 the first to retain yellow, all leaving on 13th January.

1100031-1100045	Land Rover 88" mailvan (* converted to 4-seat postbus)
1760001-1760015	Talbot Avenger 1600LS 4-seat estate car postbus
1770001-1770015	Land Rover 88" 4-seat postbus

serial	registration	chassis no.	location	route	in	out
1100045*	TSS970X	157253	Ballater	mailvan	5/82	
			Ballater	Ballater-Linn of Dee	c8/83	
			Aberdeen	reserve		by 7/91
1760001	A493WSD	343453	Brodick	Brodick-Shannochie	11/83	8/85
			Cupar	Cupar-Birkhill	8/85	6/87
1720101	JAE904X	343450	Bristol	TV Licensing	12/81	7/87
1760003	JAS291Y	343456	Ardgay	Ardgay-Strathoykel	8/82	11/85
1760004	DSW554Y	343461	Annan	Annan-Creca	10/82	1/84
1760005	DSW555Y	343643	Lockerbie	Lockerbie-Waterbeck	10/82	12/85
1760006	NBS719Y	343921	Rousay	Isle of Rousay	8/82	1/82
1760007	KAS236Y	343922	Applecross	Toscaig-Applecross	12/82	12/85
1760008	FSH121Y	343924	Duns	Duns-Abbey St.Bathans/		
				Longformacus	11/82	11/85
1760009	GSH789Y	343926	Melrose	Melrose-Maxton	5/83	2/87
1760010	USK101Y	343609	Strathy	Strathy-Strathy Point	5/83	12/85
1760011	RPS390Y	343645	Bressay	Isle of Bressay	6/83	6/87

B390TST(1100052) was supplied new with number 1170010. The bus did not find immediate use and was renumbered in the mailvan series as 1100052 before entering service as late as September 1984. 1100052 was delivered to Corby pool in April 1982 and moved to Lockerbie in December that year finally entered service in January 1985 simply re-coded as 1770052. *Mark Skillen*

1760012	DSW567Y	343646	Glenluce	Newluce-Glenluce	5/83	6/87
1760013	A587DSS	343915	Huntly	Huntly-Lumsden	10/83	10/85
1760014	GKS673Y	343916	Peebles	Peebles-Manorhead	2/83	5/87
1760015	FSB821Y	343919	Bridge of Orchy	Bridge of Orchy-Dalmally	11/82	6/87
1770001	A961ACS	157270	Brodick	Brodick-Blackwaterfoot	6/84	
			Brodick	reserve	6/91	
1100058	A497WSD	157281	Brodick	mailvan	3/84	
1770003	FSB992Y	157293	Colonsay	Isle of Colonsay	2/83	
1100004	A172TSN	157299	Pitlochry-PY3R	reserve mailvan	2/84	
1770005	RSJ836Y	157398	Brodick	reserve	4/83	
			Oban	reserve		
1100006	CNF353Y	157409	Rochdale 20 to RD20	mailvan	2/83	
1100007	YVR974Y	157421	Bury-82	mailvan	2/83	
1100050	A687RST	157427	Grantown-on-Spey	reserve (R4)	3/84	
			Inverness	mailvan	by 11/89	
1100051	A44TTS	157444	Pitlochry-PY16	mailvan	6/84	
			Grangemouth	workshop van		
1100052	B390TST	157455	Tomatin	Tomatin-Coignafearn	1/85	
			Invergarry	Invergarry-Kinlochourn	9/86	-/91
1100053	B887JSS	157467	Huntly	mailvan reserve	8/84	
			Huntly	Huntly-Clatt	1/85	5/87
			Huntly-R4	dual-purpose reserve	5/87	
			Aberdeen	reserve		by 6/93
1100054	B806WAS	157473	Lockerbie	mailvan	4/84	
			Grantown-on-Spey	Grantown-Lochindorb	5/85	6/89
			Inverness	reserve	6/89	6/91
1100055	B604UFR	157216	Ingleton-6501	mailvan	9/84	
1100056	BHN438Y	157262	Leyburn	mailvan	5/83	
			Long Preston	mailvan		
			Halifax-HXR1	mailvan		by 1/95
1770015	B144WSK	157390	Bettyhill	Bettyhill-Kinbrace	8/84	
			Thurso	reserve	6/87	8/90

1982

No 11-seat postbuses were ordered as there were still unused vehicles in storage, and as production of the Dodge Spacevan ceased early in the year, Ford, Freight-Rover and Talbot were invited to tender for future contracts, deliveries of mailvans having switched to the Leyland Sherpa in 1979. Four of the twelve Land Rovers delivered in February 1983 were converted to PSV standard after use as mailvans at the same locations, 2100011/2 were also renumbered 2770011/2. Surprisingly, a four-year old Vauxhall Chevette saloon previously used by an area sales manager was sent to Kirriemuir in May 1987 for use as a postbus despite Sierra estate cars being diverted to other duties at the time. It was soon repainted from carmine red into the correct livery and given a destination board. In July 1982 the decision was taken to recommence painting the roofs white on the Avengers, Land Rovers and Dodges at lockerbie awaiting allocation and to treat those which left in yellow on their next inspection.

2100001-2100012 Land Rover 88" 60cf. mailvan (* converted to 4-seat postbus)
2720125-2720164 Vauxhall Chevette 1300E 4-door saloon (¶ converted to 4-seat postbus)

serial	registration	chassis no.	location	route	in	out
2100003*	A942NST	174299	Inverness	dual-purpose reserve	7/83	
2100010*	A589DSS	176696	Huntly	mailvan	9/83	10/84
				Huntly-Cabrach	10/84	6/88
2100011*	A488WSD	176705	Brodick	reserve	8/83	
			Brodick	Brodick-Blackwaterfoot	11/85	6/91
2100012*	A489WSD	176772	Brodick	mailvan	8/83	
				Brodick-Kilmory	11/85	6/91
2720163	MSR101Y	111958	Perth	sales (npsv)	4/83	
			Kirriemuir-F6	Kirriemuir-Glen Prosen	5/87	c7/89

Vauxhall Chevette MSR101Y (2720163), one of many Vauxhall Chevettes bought for general duties in 1982, was later used as a postbus from Kirriemuir on the Glen Prosen route after the previous vehicle was destroyed in an accident. *P Walton*

1983

1983 similarly saw no new 11-seat buses, however all but two of a batch of Ford Sierra 1600 estate cars in cardinal red ordered in November were delivered in April 1984 and all except for the single example for Wales quickly entered service. 3760020 replaced a Land Rover as the only house with difficult access on the Dornie route was no longer occupied. 3760026 was fitted with a roof-rack.

Scottish Postal Board purchased six Ford Transits with Dormobile 16-seat bodies from Blythswood Motors of Glasgow with new type code 86, two of the batch were downseated to 12 and later 8 for the Laide-Achnasheen service; 3860004 became redundant in August 1985 due to the declining numbers of schoolchildren on the Isle of Luing.

Finally, one of the order for eighteen Land Rover 88" mailvans was converted to PSV standard when new to replace an Avenger estate car at Brodick and was renumbered 3770043.

3100041-3100058	Land Rover 88" 60cf. mailvan (* 4-seat postbus)
3760001-3760027	Ford Sierra 1600 4-seat estate-car postbus
3860001-3860006	Ford Transit postbus with Dormobile 16-seat bodywork (♥ or 12-seat plus mail)

serial	registration	chassis no.	location	route	in	out
3770043*	C486GCS	209455	Brodick	Brodick-Shannochie	8/85	6/91
3760001	A520OAS	BABNDP34437	Plockton	Plockton-Stromferry	5/84	
			Kyle of Lochalsh	Kyle-Plockton-Stromeferry	1/85	9/90
3760002	A379KKS	BABNDP34438	Kelso	Kelso-Roxburgh	6/84	3/86
3760003	A622BSF	BABNDP34439	Falkirk-RR3		-/84	
			Applecross	Applecross-Toscaig	5/85	9/90
3760004	A999HSM	BABNDP34440	Lockerbie	Lockerbie-Corrie Common	5/84	7/90

Two of the Ford Transits with Dormobile bodywork at Achnasheen station in June 1984. In the foreground is A369OST (3860001).
M. Coze

3760005	A513OAS	BABNDP34441	Dunvegan	Dunvegan-Glendale	6/84	3/90
			Portree	reserve		
3760006	A850TTS	BABNDP34442	Pitlochry-PY1R	reserve	6/84	
			Blairgowrie	Blairgowrie-Glenisla		
			Pitlochry	reserve	6/90	
			Kirriemuir	Kirriemuir-Glen Prosen	8/90	2/91
3760007	A910ESF	BABNDP34443	Anstruther-ANS2	Anstruther-Arncroach	5/84	3/92
3760008	A921RST	BABNDP34444	Dingwall	Dingwall-Heights of Dochcarty	6/84	9/90
3760009	A22HSW	BABNDP34445	Lockerbie	reserve	6/84	7/90
3760010	A920RST	BABNDP34446	Lochinver	Lochinver-Drumbeg	6/84	9/90
3760011	A922RST	BABNDP34447	Lairg	Lairg-Altass	6/84	9/90
3760012	A91PBS	BABNDP34448	Sanday	Isle of Sanday	6/84	9/90
3760013	A243MKS	BABNDP34449	Galashiels	reserve	5/84	
			Hawick-HK15	Hawick-Craik	c4/89	5/91
3760014	A621USK	BABNDP34450	Melvich	Melvich-Forsinard	7/84	
			Strathy	Strathy-Strathy Point	11/84	9/90
3760015	A410JSB	BABNDP34451	Tarbert	Tarbert-Skipness	5/85	
			Bridge of Orchy	Bridge of Orchy-Dalmally	6/87	6/91
3760016	A515OAS	BABNDP34452	Roy Bridge	Roy Bridge-Moy	5/84	7/84
			Roy Bridge	mailvan	7/84	
			Castle Douglas	Castle Douglas-Corsock	11/84	7/90
3760017	A514OAS	BABNDP34453	Dunvegan	Dunvegan-Boreraig	5/84	9/90
3760018	A92PBS	BABNDP34454	Sanday	Lady-Sanday	6/84	9/90
3760019	A971LSH	BABNDP34455	Selkirk SK19 to SK2	Selkirk-Ashkirk	5/84	2/92
3760020	A464MKS	BABNDP34456	West Linton	West Linton-Romanno Bridge	c6/84	
			Edinburgh	Regional PRO	9/85	
			Edinburgh	pool car and reserve	by 5/89	5/91
3760021	A919RST	BABNDP34457	Skerray	Skerray-Tongue	6/84	9/90
3760022	A516OAS	BABNDP34458	Killilan	Killilan-Dornie	5/84	9/90
3760023	A234EJS	BABNDP34459	Poolewe	Poolewe-Cove	6/84	
			Strathconon	Strathconon-Muir of Ord	6/87	9/90
3760024	A40RES	BABNDP34460	Kirriemuir	Kirriemuir-Glen Prosen	5/94	
			Forres	Forres-Braemoray	7/86	-/89
3760025	A21HSW	BABNDP34461	Annan	Annan-Creca	6/84	7/90
3760026	A656RAS	BABNDP34462	Kyle of Lochalsh	reserve	6/84	
			Applecross	Applecross-Kishorn	12/85	9/90
3760027	B244ADW	BABNDP34463	Usk	Usk-Llandenny	1/85	9/91
			Usk	mailcar	9/91	
3860001♥	A369OST	29473	Laide	Laide-Achnasheen	2/84	5/90
3860002♥	A370OST	32631	Laide	reserve	2/84	8/91
3860003	A943VGG	32639	Killin-C21	Killin-Callander	4/84	8/90
3860004	A409JSB	32630	Luing	Isle of Luing	1/84	8/85
			Elgol	Elgol-Broadford	10/85	7/90
3860005	A121SGA	32638	Dunoon	Dunoon-Tighnabruaich	1/84	by 8/91
3860006	A320EJS	32632	Timsgarry	Timsgarry-Stornoway	5/84	
			Stornoway	reserve		8/91

Jack Wahlberg and David Cott spent four summers travelling to and on all the Scottish Postbuses in aid of the Imperial Cancer Research Fund. David is seen beside his preserved Sierra estate Postbus A971LSH (3760019) outside the "Last House" at John O'Groats.
JP Wahlberg

51

1984

With the demise of the Dodge Spacevan orders were placed for fifty-six Dormobile 11-seat conversions based on the wide-bodied Freight Rover Sherpa 285 that had been introduced the previous year as a 320cf. mailvan. They had five-speed gearboxes, grey vinyl passenger seats, front fog lamps and a heater in the passenger compartment. Those for Scotland passed through Falkirk pool like the Sierras the previous year, rather than Lockerbie. 4750013 was delivered to Alnwick before moving all the way to Surrey for service, and 4750010 was registered by Post Office HQ in connection with the 350th Anniversary celebrations at Bagshot Park in 1985. 4750007/13 were later fitted with automatic gearboxes by South Eastern Postal Region. 4750028 was renumbered 4780028 and reduced to four seats for use by the South Western Public Relations Office. Scottish Postal Board purchased a further Ford Transit with Dormobile 16-seat body.

Reflecting the trial of seventy Austin Maestro mailvans the choice of car-based postbuses was for twenty Austin Maestro hatchbacks, delivered in dark red; the Scottish examples were repainted at Falkirk. The smaller capacity of the hatchbacks caused problems on some routes that had previously been operated by Avenger and Sierra estates with roof racks, and various three-way exchanges took place to overcome this. Later two Ford Escort hatchbacks from the year's delivery of thirty-three driver training cars in rosso red with lorenzo grey interior trim were pressed into service as postbuses.

4720192-4720224	Ford Escort 1100 Popular 3-door driver-instruction hatchback
4750001-4750056	Freight-Rover Sherpa K4 285 11-seat postbus with Dormobile conversion
	(▲ 9-seats or † 4-seat crewbus)
4760001-4760020	Austin Maestro 1.6L 5-door hatchback postbus
4860001	Ford Transit with Dormobile B16F bodywork .

serial	registration	chassis no.	location	route	in	out
4720193	C748PSX	25668	Perth	driver-trainer	10/85	
			Dunblane-S12	Dunblane-Braco	by 12/88	3/92
4720209	B510KSC	25667	Crieff	driver-trainer	6/85	
			Dollar-S44	Dollar-Glendevon	c11/90	
4750001	B154CEP	239241	Llanidloes 8 to L8	Llanidloes-Llangurig	7/85	1/92
4750002	B794YFR	240939	Ulverston	Ulverston-Grizedale Forest	5/85	
			Barrow-R2016	reserve	by 4/89	2/92
4750003	B461NSB	239566	Portnahaven	Islay-Portnahaven	5/85	
			Port Ellen	reserve		1/92
4750004	B321VST	241419	Alligin	Alligin-Kinlochewe	4/85	
			Dingwall	reserve	early -/89	2/92

Opposite, top:- **The first Sherpa Postbus to gain the current livery was B267 VOU (4750025). It was originally used by the South Western Postal Region PRO before allocation to the only route in Cornwall which runs from Wadebridge to Penrose. It is pictured pausing at Treburrick in July 1990.** *D A Cott*
Opposite, bottom:- **Twenty Austin Maestro cars were ordered for Postbuses in 1984. These were never very popular with the drivers, but the lettering fitted the bodywork well - even when bi-lingual. Here is shown B105HJS (4760003) which was allocated to the Bernera-Callanish route on the Isle of Harris.**
Ken Ross collection

4750005	B600YHV	240916	Reigate-69	Reigate-Leigh	3/85	
			Redhill-954	reserve	c7/88	2/92
4750006	B675GVK	240936	Chathill	Chathill-Bamburgh	3/85	
			Alnwick-R4	reserve	by 8/88	
			Morpeth			8/92
4750007	B473KNJ	241207	Redhill 68 to 951	Redhill-Outwood	3/85	10/91
4750008	B676GVK	241281	Rothbury-4	Rothbury-Alwinton	7/85	10/91
4750009	C620JHS	241261	Strathaven-M44	Strathaven-Dungavel	3/86	8/91
4750010	B601YHV	241181	Oxted 15 to 953	Oxted-Lingfield	3/85	10/91
4750011	B525ARN	240902	Broughton-in-Furness 2103 Broughton -Cockley Beck		6/85	2/92
4750012	B777MSM	240908	Lockerbie (PBR1)	reserve	3/85	2/92
4750013	B486MAP	241254	Chichester	driver-trainer	7/85	
			Dorking	Dorking-Ockley	8/85	
			Reigate 2 to 952	Reigate-Leigh	c7/88	10/91
4750014	B449VAS	241274	Elgol	Elgol-Broadford	3/85	
			Falkirk-FK33R	reserve	12/85	10/90
4750015	B526ARN	241546	Barrow-in-Furness	reserve	6/85	
			Ulverston-2412	Ulverston-Grizedale Forest		2/92
4750016	C876TKS	241279	Melrose-MR7	Galashiels-Lilliesleaf	3/86	
			Melrose-MR7	Melrose-Lilliesleaf		2/92
			Livingston-LV24	crewbus		9/93
4750017	B652LAO	241581	Penrith	Penrith-Martindale	7/85	
			Kirkcudbright (PB87)	Kirkcudbright-Borgue	7/87	2/92
4750018	B359DGG	241557	Denny FK24 to FK31	Denny-Fintry	3/85	10/90
			Falkirk-FK33	crewbus	10/90	by 9/91
4750019	B155CEP	241596	Llanidloes 7 to L7	Llanidloes-Dylife	6/85	1/92
4750020	B653LAO	242522	Penrith	reserve	7/85	
			Penrith	Penrith-Martindale	7/87	12/90
			Thornhill-PB23	Thornhill-Moniaive	1/91	2/92
4750021	B150YTT	241987	Honiton	Honiton-Luppitt	7/85	3/92
4750022	B36DGD	242556	Aberfoyle S49	Aberfoyle-Kinlochard	4/85	3/92
			to S11			
4750023	B715LWV	242615	Newbury NE47-N56	reserve	8/85	12/87
			Basingstoke-PB3	crewbus		
4750024	B372LCD	242593	Sittingbourne-341	Sittingbourne-Wormshill	4/85	10/91
4750025	B267VOU	243395	Bristol	Regional PRO	5/85	
			Wadebridge-5	Wadebridge-Penrose	9/85	3/92
4750026	B321MSC	243054	West Calder	West Calder-Tarbrax	4/85	1/92
4750027	B397DGA	243322	Clarkston	Clarkston-Carmunnock	4/85	7/88
			Llandrindod Wells-LD1	Llandrindod Wells-Rhayader	11/88	
			Llandrindod Wells	reserve	1/92	3/92
			Builth Wells	Builth Wells-Painscastle		8/92
4780028†	B268VOU	243301	Bristol	Regional PRO	5/85	by 9/89
4750029	B716LWV	244352	Hungerford (PB2)	Hungerford-Great Shefford	7/85	11/87
			Basingstoke-PB2	crewbus		
4750030	B850MSW	243354	Lockerbie (PB13)	Lockerbie-St. Ann's	6/85	2/92
4750031	C516JJS	243388	Lochmaddy	Lochmaddy-Sidinish	9/85	2/92
4750032	B193NSM	244364	Castle Douglas	reserve	7/85	
			Penrith	Penrith-Martindale		
			Castle-Douglas (PBR2)	reserve		2/92
4750033	B311CGG	243082	Biggar-M54	Biggar-Tweedsmuir	4/85	11/86
4750034	B725XSN	242995	Crieff-C3R	reserve	4/85	
			Perth-PR10	reserve	8/87	3/92
4750035	B191NSM	244382	Thornhill	Thornhill-Moniaive	7/85	1/91
4750036	B206HJS	243392	Lochmaddy	Lochmaddy-Airport	7/85	
			Portree	reserve	7/91	2/92
			Lochboisdale	reserve		6/92
4750037	B697LWV	244156	Tunbridge Wells-200 Tunbridge Wells-Mayfield		5/85	2/92
4750038	B511YDS	244386	Tiree	Isle of Tiree	5/85	8/88
			Urmston-90	crewbus	by 12/90	12/91
4750039	B244HJS	243409	Lochboisdale	reserve	6/85	
			Tigharry	Tigharry-Airport		
			Portree	reserve		2/92
4750040	C528PSB	243303	Port Askaig	Port Askaig	9/85	8/91
			Glasgow	crewbus		by 11/91
4750041	B713WAS	244354	Strathconon	Strathconon-Muir of Ord	5/85	
			Newtonmore	Newtonmore-Kinlochlaggan	6/87	
			Lochboisdale	reserve	c11/88	
			Castlebay	Castlebay-Eoligarry		2/92

Several vehicles entered Post Office service on other duties and became postbuses later in their Royal Mail life. Escort saloon B510KSC (4720209) was originally a driver-training car at Crieff. For a short time it was allocated to the Dollar-Glendevon route where it was photographed in November 1990. The number S44 underneath the Escort badge is the local running number for this duty. *P Walton*

4750042	C738PSX	244390	Edinburgh	Regional PRO	10/85	
			Pitlochry	Pitlochry-Rannoch Station	1/89	
			Falkirk-FK006	reserve		by 9/91
4750043	B718WAS	244798	Nairn	Nairn-Glenferness	5/85	3/92
4750044	B445KSX	244148	Dunbar	Dunbar-Innerwick	5/85	
			Haddington-HBRD	reserve	12/87	2/92
			Edinburgh	crewbus	spring -/92	6/92
4750045	B917RKS	244296	Galashiels-GLR4	reserve	6/85	1/92
			Livingston	crewbus	spring -/92	by 9/92
4750046	B682WAS	244795	Portree R5	reserve	5/85	
			Kyle-R5	reserve	8/87	2/92
4750047	B919MSC	244116	Kirriemuir-F5	Kirriemuir-Glen Clova	5/85	
			Forfar-F4R	reserve	12/87	
			Dundee	reserve	10/91	3/92
4750048	B310MFS	244369	Cupar-CP1	Cupar-Peat Inn	6/85	3/92
4750049	B373LCD	244393	Canterbury (39)-440	Canterbury-Crundale	4/85	3/92
4750050	B45DYS	244124	Callander-S37	Callander-Trossachs	4/85	3/92
4750051	C802JJS	244902	Castlebay	Castlebay-Borve	10/85	
			Lochboisdale	reserve		6/92
4750052	B607NSB	244129	Oban	reserve	5/85	1/92
4750053	B254MSW	244111	Annan (PB64)	Annan-Powfoot	4/85	2/92
4750054	B856WSK	244288	Thurso	Thurso-Wick Airport	7/85	2/92
4750055▲	B444XES	244257	Blairgowrie-P83	Blairgowrie-Glenshee	6/85	
			Annan	Annan-Powfoot		3/92
4750056	B153CEP	244181	Llandrindod Wells	reserve	6/85	
			Aberystwyth	Aberystwyth-Cwmystwyth	7/86	9/86
			Llandrindod Wells	reserve	9/86	by 4/92

4760001	B759WAS	299127	Forres	Forres-Braemoray	5/85	
			Kirriemuir	Kirriemuir-Glen Prosen	7/86	
			Perth	car (npsv)	5/87	
			Kirriemuir	Kirriemuir-Glen Prosen	c7/89	8/90
4760002	B714WAS	299141	Lairg	reserve	5/85	
			Inverness	Inverness-Coignafearn	9/86	5/91
4760003	B105HJS	299123	Bernera	Bernera-Callanish	5/85	5/91
4760004	B683WAS	298972	Newtonmore	Newtonmore-Kinlochlaggan	5/85	3/86
4760005	B809ORS	299130	Aboyne	Aboyne-Logie Coldstone	6/85	2/92
4760006	B715WAS	298989	Scourie	Scourie-Kylestrome	5/85	12/86
4760007	B711WAS	299121	Kyle of Lochalsh		6/85	
			Falkirk-RR3	reserve	by 8/95	
			Kelso-KO3	Kelso-Roxburgh	4/86	
			Galashiels	reserve	by 3/89	4/92
4760008	B742DNS	299143	Balfron	Balfron-Fintry	5/85	6/91
			Aboyne			
4760009	B937DUS	299165	Dunblane-S12	Dunblane-Braco	5/85	by 12/88
			Grangemouth			3/91
4760010	B412XES	298666	Pitlochry-PY11	Pitlochry-Dalnaspidal	6/85	11/90
4760011	B916RKS	299194	Hawick	Hawick-Craik	6/85	
			Kelso-KO3	Kelso-Roxburgh		
			Galashiels-GLR5	reserve	c4/89	c2/92
4760012	B712WAS	298978	Invergordon	Invergordon-Kildermorie	5/85	10/86
4760013	B413XES	299136	Birnam-PY10	Aberfeldy-Birnam	6/85	by 9/91
4760014	B915RKS	299205	Kelso-KO4	Kelso-Smailholm/Hassington	6/85	4/92
4760015	B606NSB	299183	Oban	reserve	5/85	2/92
4760016	B196ORS	298893	Turriff	Turriff-Fyvie	6/85	12/88
			Elgin	car (npsv)		by 12/89
4760017	B741MSX	298986	Kinross-K7	Kinross-Rumbling Bridge	5/85	7/90
4760018	B941DUS	299280	Dollar-S44	Dollar-Glendevon	5/85	by 11/90
4760019	C737PSX	299209	West Linton-WL4	West Linton-Romanno Bridge	9/85	
			Peebles	Peebles-Manorhead	2/87	
			West Linton-WL4	West Linton-Romanno Bridge	6/87	4/91
4760020	C371KFF	299082	Machynlleth-MH16	Machynlleth-Aberhosan	10/85	by 7/91
4860001	A916RST	BDVPER38588	Lairg	Talmine-Tongue-Lairg	6/84	8/91

There is a very steep and narrow entrance to the small yard behind Wooler Post Office, which has many scrapes in the wall caused by wing mirrors, firstly at Commer height and later at Montego level. The routes now only call there, operating out of Alnwick. C640 NCN (5760016) and C642 NCN (5760018) are seen in the yard. C640NCN carried a MG grill in 1990. *D A Cott*

1985

A Talbot Express 12-seater was bought as a Scottish regional reserve; it was tested on the Blairgowrie to Glenshee route but was returned to Falkirk pool as unsuitable, it was found to be too wide for the driveway at Aberfeldy and was used briefly at Aberfoyle in August 1985. It passed to Scottish Postal Board Public Relations being noted on loan to Scottish Opera in February 1986, Commonwealth Games sponsorship in July 1986, Scottish Opera Go Around in August 1986, Borders Festival at Selkirk in September 1987 and Marmelade Productions in March 1988.

The main delivery was for thirty-three Freight Rover Sherpas, this time with 11-seat conversion by Besco featuring a grab handle by the nearside door to facilitate entry. 5750034 operated at Post Office HQ with registration C275 BYW. In connection with sponsorship of the Commonwealth Games the mesh partition was removed and two flag mountings were fitted to the roof as it was to transport the baton carriers, however an urgent need for a replacement bus at Louth resulted in Talbot Express 5750001 attending the Games instead and the Sherpa returned to Kidbrooke for restoration to PSV status. When it reached Lincolnshire it was found to be carrying duplicated plates and was therefore given a new registration.

Car-based buses included another fifteen Austin Maestro hatchbacks for Scotland together with four of the larger Austin Montego estate cars to replace Dodge 11-seaters in Northumbria which entered service in a darker, almost maroon colour. Maestro 5760015 began at Kidbrooke but was sent to Scotland to replace similar 4760012 which was destroyed in a collision on Balacraggan level crossing - luckily the Postwoman driver suffered only scratches and bruises. A Ford Fiesta hatchback diesel mailcar from a delivery of 600 was PSV-certified from new to replace the wrecked Maestro 4760004 on the very poorly patronised service from Newtonmore to Kinlochlaggan. After its withdrawal in September 1990 the Post Office recognised the interest in what could be the smallest PSV ever and retained it for the Heritage Fleet. In January 1991 when the reserve Sierra working Kirriemuir to Glen Prosen was damaged in an accident, another Fiesta mailcar from the same batch, 5920271, previously repainted unmarked white on TV Licence Investigation work was resprayed red as a replacement, while a sister car was transferred for the Dollar to Glendevon route. At least two others from the batch were used as stand-ins at Louth and Rothbury.

Scottish Postal Board expressed a wish to phase out Land Rover postbuses as they were unpopular with passengers and expensive to operate. Postbuses on the Isle of Skye received bi-lingual Gaelic lettering - Bus A'Phuist Rioghail - in October 1985, and vehices in other parts of the Highlands and Islands followed.

5750001	Talbot Express 1300 12-seat postbus
5750002-5750034	Freight-Rover Sherpa K4 12-seat postbus (Besco conversion)
5760001-5760015	Austin Maestro 1.6L 4-seat hatchback postbus
5760016-5760019	Austin Montego 1.6 4-seat estate car postbus
5920001-5920600	Ford Fiesta 1.6 4-seat hatchback diesel mailcar

serial	registration	chassis no.	location	route	in	out
5750001	B85MSC	209210	Edinburgh	Regional Reserve	7/85	8/85
				to PRO (npsv)	by 2/86	2/91
5750002	C85JSD	256156	Falkirk-FK32	reserve	3/86	
			Grangemouth	reserve		6/93
5750003	C701KJS	256076	Tigharry	Tigharry-Airport	4/86	
			Stornoway	reserve		
			Timsgarry	Timsgarry-Callanish		2/92
5750004	C866UFS	256034	Leven	Leven-New Gilston	3/86	1/92
			Livingston	crewbus	by 4/92	
5750005	C557KJS	256558	Castlebay	Castlebay-Eoligarry	3/86	3/92
5750006	C516GGE	256098	Dunoon	reserve	2/86	
			Biggar	Biggar-Tweedsmuir	4/87	8/91
			Paisley-313	crewbus		by 11/91
5750007	C224XST	256168	Dingwall	reserve	2/86	
			Alligin	Alligin-Kinlochewe	early 1989	2/92
5750008	C491SSF	255915	Haddington-HDB	Haddington-Garvald	3/86	
			Edinburgh	reserve	spring 1992	by 6/92
5750009	C497SSF	256362	Gorebridge	Gorebridge-Moorfoot	3/86	1/92
			Edinburgh	city crewbus reserve	spring 1992	by 6/92
5750010	C697ATS	256498	Aberfeldy-PY6	Aberfeldy-Glen Lyon-Lubreoch	3/86	3/92
5750011	C388PSM	256516	Castle Douglas	Castle Douglas-Mossdale	3/86	2/92
5750012	C878TKS	256675	Hawick-HK16	Hawick-Bonchester Bridge	3/86	2/92
			Livingston-LV26	crewbus		by 6/93
5750013	C370RSB	256591	Port Ellen	reserve	3/86	8/91
5750014	C877TKS	256555	Kelso-KO2	Kelso-Stichill	3/86	1/92
			Edinburgh	lcrewbus	spring 1992	by 6/92
5750015	C694ATS	256442	Crianlarich-C22	Crianlarich-Killin	2/86	
			Perth-PR11	reserve	3/92	
5750016	C541VSC	256638	Linlithgow	Linlithgow-Blackness	3/86	2/92
			Livingston	crewbus	spring 1992	by 6/92
5750017	C531PSB	256725	Bowmore	Bowmore-Port Askaig	2/86	8/91
5750018	C222XST	256721	Lairg	reserve	2/86	2/92
5750019	C513PFG	256891	Newbury	Newbury-West Ilsley	2/86	1/88
			Basingstoke-PB4	crewbus		by -/93
5750020	C512PFG	256976	Hungerford	Hungerford-Kintbury	6/86	12/87
			Newbury-N56	crewbus		by -/93
5750021	C514PFG	257227	Henley-HT15	Henley-Frieth	2/86	3/88
			Wokingham-PC2	crewbus	c3/90	
5750022	C551PFG	257324	Petersfield-P21	Petersfield-Froxfield	2/86	3/92
5750023	C523RYJ	257080	Newport, IoW	Regional Reserve	6/86	
			Sandown-74	crewbus	by 7/88	by 4/92
5750024	C543PFG	257012	Redhill	reserve	2/86	by 7/88
			Dorking 2 to 955	Dorking-Ockley	c7/88	3/92
5750025	C574RYJ	257115	Newbury	Newbury-Chaddleworth	6/86	
			Newbury (N55R)	reserve	1/88	
			Basingstoke	crewbus	by 7/91	3/92
5750026	C549PFG	257857	Newport, IoW	Newport-Newtown	2/86	
			(later-21)	crewbus	by 7/88	
5750027	C550PFG	257418	Newport, IoW	Newport-Brighstone	3/86	
			(later-22)	crewbus	by 7/88	
5750028	C371RSB	258185	Inveraray	Inveraray-Dalmally	3/86	8/91

Opposite, top:- **Some postbuses are rarely photographed, largely due to their inaccessibility to mainland dwelling camera-owners. One such is C231RBS (5760007), captured outside the driver's house on the Isle of Rousay.** *P J Cott*

Opposite, bottom:- **Talbot Express 1300 postbus B85MSC (5750001) was donated by the Post Office to the Corstorphine Rotary Club for further use as a Community Bus. It is seen here in February 1991 with appropriate markings.** *P Walton*

5750029	C372RSB	258046	Oban	reserve	4/86	
			Luing	Isle of Luing	12/87	
			Tiree	Isle of Tiree	c8/88	8/91
5750030	D586ASX	258076	Falkirk	driver-trainer	8/86	
			Edinburgh	crewbus		
			Aberdeen	crewbus		
			Dunfermline-33	crewbus	spring 1992	
5750031	D956SSM	258042	Castle Douglas (PB54)	Castle Douglas-Auchencairn	8/86	2/92
5750032	C867UFS	258087	Cupar-R4	reserve	3/86	
			Dunfermline-30	crewbus	spring 1992	3/92
5750033	C621JHS	258146	Biggar	reserve	2/86	
			Biggar	Biggar-Newbiggin	8/91	
			Dunoon	Dunoon-Tighnabruaich	by 9/91	by 11/91
5750034	D65OWA	253971	Louth-L8	Louth-Goulceby	10/86	1/92
5760001	C216XST	354229	Killilan	Killilan-Dornie	12/85	9/90
5760002	C218XST	354222	Ardgay	Ardgay-Strathoykel	11/85	
			Poolewe	Poolewe-Cove	6/87	5/91
5760003	C146OSW	354232	Lockerbie	Lockerbie-Waterbeck	12/85	7/90
5760004	C147OSW	354225	Lockerbie	Lockerbie-Hightae	12/85	7/90
5760005	C336WMS	354206	Falkirk-FK31	reserve	12/85	by 3/92
5760006	C150KJS	354537	Lochboisdale	reserve	1/86	
			Grantown-on-Spey	Grantown-Lochindorb	6/89	
			Melvich	Melvich-Kinbrace	6/91	3/92
5760007	C231RBS	354240	Rousay	Isle of Rousay	12/85	5/91
5760008	C217XST	354339	Kylesku	Kylesku-Elphin	12/85	5/91
5760009	C838TSF	354235	Cupar	Cupar-Newburgh	12/85	3/92
5760010	C871TKS	354552	Duns-DS3	Duns-Abbey St. Bathans/		
				Longformacus	11/85	3/92
5760011	C926RSA	354549	Huntly	Huntly-Lumsden	11/85	12/91
5760012	C26GGE	354381	Abington-M76	Abington-Crawfordjohn	11/85	9/90
5760013	C837TSF	354532	Cupar	Cupar-Brunton	12/85	3/92
5760014	C385XSK	354540	Kinbrace	Kinbrace-Forsinard	12/85	5/91
5760015	C280BYW	354544	Kidbrooke	(for tests)	4/86	
			Invergordon	Invergordon-Kildermorie	12/86	3/92
5760016	C640NCN	229207	Alnwick	Alnwick-Alnham	1/86	
			Wooler	Wooler-Kirknewton	4/90	6/91
5760017	C641NCN	217435	Wooler	Wooler-Kirknewton	1/86	4/90
5760018	C642NCN	240698	Wooler	Wooler-Doddington	1/86	
			Morpeth	Morpeth-Whalton	4/91	6/91
5760019	C643NCN	222274	Morpeth	reserve	1/86	
			Rothbury	Rothbury-Biddlestone	1/88	7/91
5920014	D965TTN	47014	Morpeth	mailcar	8/86	
			Rothbury	Rothbury-Alwinton	8/89	8/89
			Morpeth	mailcar		
5920162	D56OWA	50890	Louth L10	mailcar	8/86	
			Louth	Louth-Goulceby	8/88	
			Louth-10	mailcar		
5920270	C712ATS	51787	Dundee 4 to D4	mailcar	4/86	
			Dollar-S103	Dollar-Glendevon	3/92	
			Dingwall	reserve	by 8/92	
			Perth	customer care car	by 8/93	
5920271	C270RSF	51788	Falkirk	TV Licensing van	2/85	
			Kirriemuir-F6	Kirriemuir-Glen Prosen	1/91	3/92
			Dundee			8/94
5920351	D454DAS	51868	Newtonmore	Newtonmore-Kinlochlaggan	8/86	
			Inverness	Inverness-Killen Lodge	6/87	8/90
			PHQ	Archive fleet	by 9/90	Current
5920528	D966TTN	59534	Morpeth-24	mailcar	9/86	
			Rothbury	Rothbury-Alwinton	10/86	10/86
			Morpeth-24	mailcar		
5920544	C410NTN	59550	Alnwick 20 to R3	mailcar	4/86	9/89
			Wooler	Wooler routes	9/89	9/89
			Alnwick-12	mailcar	9/89	

1986

A batch of twenty Freight-Rover Sherpa vans was purchased and converted to 11-seat postbuses at Bamber Bridge, completion running from July 1987 to January 1988. 6750008 was sent to Kidbrooke for evaluation and used as a crewbus at Acton in west London. It was then used on driver training in Wensleydale before being sent to work Laide to Achnasheen in place of the unreliable Ford Transits; it carried small Royal Mail Post Bus lettering as used on estate cars.

After the unsatisfactory use of hatchbacks, car purchases returned to the Ford Sierra estate with sixteen petrol and a single diesel-engined model although not all found use as buses, the first being used by DSD Racing as support for the Swiftair Racing Team, going to Le Mans in summer 1987. Seven others were used as non-PSVs and 6760007/12/5/6 were renumbered 6720145/47/46/55. Evaluation vehicle 6760014 was destroyed by fire and its registration is subject to confirmation. 6760006 replaced Maestro 4760006 on the Scourie service, another accident victim.

Thirteen Land Rover 90 vans were delivered in April and May 1987 and converted to PSV standard, most carried incorrect registrations in D-SAS before entering service, which in the case of 6770009 was not until November 1987. The newly-formed Edinburgh district reintroduced the white foor for postbuses under its control, applying it to vehicles already in service.

6750001-6750020	Freight-Rover Sherpa 285 11-seat postbus (Bamber Bridge conversion)
6760001-6760016	Ford Sierra 1.6 petrol 4-seat estate car postbus
6760017	Ford Sierra 2.3DL diesel 4-seat estate car postbus
6770001-6770013	Land Rover 90 4-seat postbus

serial	registration	chassis no.	location	route	in	out
6750001	E469PKG	806136	Abergavenny-10	Abergavenny-Skenfrith	9/87	5/92
6750002	E218VUJ	806651	Aberystwyth AH	Aberystwyth-Blaenpennal	9/87	c12/92
6750003	E158REP	806121	Llandovery 7 to LY7	Llandovery-Myddfai/Covington	9/87	7/93
6750004	E964PWY	806116	Ripon	Ripon-Masham	9/87	6/88
			Newtown-R	Newtown reserve	6/89	
			Newtown	Newtown-New Mills	9/90	
			Newtown-R	Newtown reserve		c12/92
6750005	E206WGB	806142	Biggar	reserve	7/87	
			Lanark	reserve	-/90	5/91
6750006	E233HSL	806084	Aberfeldy	Aberfeldy-Lawers	11/87	
			Pitlochry	reserve		
			Aberfeldy-PY5	Aberfeldy-Lawers		3/92
6750007	E234HSL	806594	Kirriemuir-F5	Kirriemuir-Glen Clova	12/87	3/92
6750008	E461KYL	806105	Letters HQ	Kidbrooke	8/87	
			Acton	crewbus	by 10/89	
			Northallerton	driver-trainer		
			Dingwall	reserve	by 8/90	c7/91
			Lochmaddy	Lochmaddy-Airport		
			Lochboisdale	reserve		3/92
6750009	E232HSL	806131	Aberfoyle-S9	Aberfoyle-Inversnaid	11/87	3/92
6750010	E224AJR	806146	Morpeth	reserve	10/87	
			Chathill	Chathill-Bamburgh	by 8/88	
			Alnwick			8/92

6750011	E354JSC	806237	Dunbar-DBB	Dunbar-Innerwick	12/87	
			Edinburgh-PBR	reserve	1/92	9/92
			Dunfermline-30	crewbus		
6750012	E220VUJ	806523	Builth Wells	Builth Wells-Abergwesyn	10/87	
			Llandrindod Wells-R	reserve	4/92	c12/92
6750013	E221VUJ	806222	Llandrindod Wells	Llandrindod Wells-Llaithddu	10/87	
			Llandrindod Wells	Llandrindod Wells-Rhayader	1/92	2/93
6750014	E613CGM	806241	Hungerford H30	Hungerford-East Garston	11/87	3/92
6750015	E614CGM	806242	Hungerford-H31	Hungerford-Kintbury	12/87	
			Newbury	reserve	by 7/91	3/92
6750016	E484WFC	806824	Aylesbury	crewbus	11/87	
			High Wycombe	crewbus		
6750017	E229VUJ	806652	Newtown	Newtown-New Mills	12/87	
			Aberystwyth	Aberystwyth-Cwmystwyth	9/90	
			Newtown-N24	Newtown-New Mills		c12/92
6750018	E230VUJ	806341	Builth Wells-BS5	Builth Wells-Painscastle	1/88	
			Builth Wells-BS12	Builth Wells-Abergwesyn		c12/92
6750019	E644CGM	806291	Newbury N57 to NB2	Newbury-West Ilsley	1/88	3/92
6750020	E645CGM	806327	Newbury-N58	Newbury-Chaddleworth	1/88	3/92
6760001	D57FYR	HD15688	Postal Headquarters	Swiftair Racing Team (npsv)		
6760002	D895BKS	HD15689	Melrose MR4	Melrose-Maxton	5/87	
			Galashiels-GLR5	reserve	5/92	7/92
6760003	D735UHH	HD15690	Glenluce	Glenluce-New Luce	6/87	
			Dumfries	car (npsv)	by 9/90	7/90
6760004	D894BKS	HD15691	Peebles-PB11	Peebles-Manorhead	5/87	5/92
6760005	D981EFS	HD15692	Cupar	Cupar-Birkhill	6/87	5/92
6760006	D687FAS	HD15693	Scourie	Scourie-Kylestrome	6/87	
			Lairg	reserve	7/92	8/93
6720145	D264WAO	HD15694	Carlisle	npsv		
6760008	E854KNH	HD15695	Milton Keynes	Training College (npsv)		by 6/89
6760009	E901CSA	HD15696	Aberdeen	Marketing (npsv)	6/87	
			Forres	Forres-Braemoray	mid -/89	2/92
6760010	D67FYR	HD15697	International Letters	London (npsv)		
6760011	D572YSA	HD15698	Banchory	Banchory-Ballater	6/87	2/92
6720147	E469AAO	HD15699	Carlisle	(npsv)	9/87	
6760013	D573YSA	HD15700	Bressay	Isle of Bressay	6/87	7/92
			Perth	(npsv)		
6760014	D56FYR	HD15701	Postal Headquarters	Kidbrooke		
			International Letters	London (npsv)		-/87
6720146	E518PUB	HD15702	Bradford	Bradford (npsv)	8/87	
6720144	D114TDV	HD15703	South Wales & South			
			West Parcels	Plymouth (Sales car - npsv)		
6760017	D920TGE	07769	Dalmally	Tarbert-Skipness	6/87	7/92
6770001	D283YRS	289791	Ballater	Ballater-Linn of Dee	5/87	12/92
6770002	D282YRS	289795	Huntly	Huntly-Clatt	5/87	12/92
6770003	D676FAS	289799	Bettyhill	Bettyhill-Kinbrace	6/87	8/90
			Lairg	reserve	9/90	by 2/95
6770004	D677FAS	289800	Halkirk	Halkirk-Altnabreac	6/87	
			Thurso	reserve and workshop van	8/90	11/92
6770005	D678FAS	289803	Altnaharra	Altnaharra-Hispond	5/87	11/92
6770006	D679FAS	289807	Rogart	Rogart-Sciberscross	5/87	11/92
6770007	D680FAS	289826	Arnisdale	Arnisdale-Kyle	5/87	
			Kyle of Lochalsh	reserve	8/90	12/92
6770008	D681FAS	289829	Dalwhinnie	Dalwhinnie-Drummin	5/87	
			Invergarry	Invergarry-Kinlochourn	6/91	11/92
			Fort William	reserve		
6770009	D682FAS	289831	Rogart	Rogart-West Langwell	11/87	11/92
6770010	D683FAS	289833	Grantown-on-Spey	reserve	6/87	
			Fort William	reserve		12/92
6770011	D684FAS	289837	Ardgay	Ardgay-Craigs	5/87	
			Ardgay	Ardgay-Strathoykel	6/91	11/92
6770012	D686FAS	289841	Drumnadrochit	Drumnadrochit-Grotaig	5/87	
			Dingwall	reserve	6/91	12/92
			Grangemouth	workshop recovery vehicle (npsv)	by 4/93	by 2/95
6770013	D685FAS	289845	Ardgay	Ardgay-Strathoykel	6/87	
			Ardgay	Ardgay-Craigs	6/91	11/92

D679FAS (6770006) was one of the thirteen Land Rovers bought in 1987, shown here on the Rogart to Sciberscross service. *M.S. Thompson*

One of the Ford Fiestas used as postbuses was D454DAS (5920351), later preserved by the Post Office. It was photographed in September 1986 when in use on the Newtonmore to Kinlochlaggan service, replacing a written-off Maestro that in turn replaced a Dodge. The route was soon upgraded to a Sherpa. *P Walton*

1987

Ordered in 1987 two twin-wheel Freight-Rover Sherpa 310s were delivered in June and July 1988 and converted to 14 seat postbuses at Bamber Bridge. 7750001 with a standard low roof was given Gaelic bilingual livery and fitted with registration plates lettered 'BUS 50' for a ceremony at Inverness in April 1988 where the Chairman of the Post Office handed over the keys to mark the fiftieth service in the Highlands and Islands. The bus later entered service on Ripon-Masham where a larger vehicle was badly needed - the route made £4,000 profit in its first five years and the bus often ran full. The County Council requested a 19-seater but the Post Office was unwilling to provide a driver qualified to drive a single-decker rather than holding a class III minibus licence, and even the larger Sherpa often left passengers standing. The second of the pair featured a raised roof and was ordered for the Isle of Luing, where the school population had again increased, presumably in height as well as number.

Twenty-four Land Rover Defender 90 mailvans delivered between May and July 1988 were given serials in the postbus sequence, three were corrected by Glasgow workshop before entering service but the others retained their 77 type codes.

A batch of twenty-four Land Rover mailvans carried postbus serials in error but F471OHT (7770022) found a different use with the South West PRO as a support vehicle for the Post office hot-air balloon team. It is photographed at Arley in May 1990 coupled to the balloon trailer carrying balloon registration G-NVPR.
D A Cott

Later, due to a shortage of replacement vehicles a Ford Escort three-door mailcar and two five-door hatchbacks purchased for Post Office Counters were transferred to postbus duties, two of the latter operating in unmarked Ford blue. When the Peugeot estate car on the Kelso-Smailholm route was written off after an accident in 1993 a further Escort car was used as an emergency replacement.

7690001-7690080	Ford Escort 1.6L diesel 3-door mailcar
7720094-7720143	Ford Escort 1.6L petrol 5-door hatchback car
7720311-7720392	Ford Escort 1.6DL diesel 5-door hatchback car
7730040-7730171	Ford Sierra 1.6L hatchback car
7750001-7750002	Freight-Rover Sherpa 310 lwb 14-seat postbus (Bamber Bridge conversion)
7770001-7770024	Land Rover 90 60cf. mailvan

serial	registration	chassis no.	location	route	in	out
7690056	E529YNT		Aberystwyth	mailcar	5/88	
			Machynlleth	Machynlleth-Aberhosan	8/91	3/92
7720099	E418KTS		Dundee Counters	(npsv)	c6/88	
			Dollar	Dollar-Glendevon	by 9/91	
			Perth	(npsv)	3/92	by 2/95
7720101	E419KTS		Dundee Counters	(npsv)	c6/88	
			Birnam	Birnam-Aberfeldy	by 7/91	
			Falkirk	(npsv)	3/92	by 2/95
7720365	F555SFS	BBAAJG72356	Edinburgh	city (npsv)	8/88	
			Kelso	Kelso-Smailholm/Hassington	c6/93	
			Edinburgh			10/94
7730129	F543OAS		Inverness	(npsv)	late -/88	
			Inverness	Inverness-Gorthleck	c8/90	9/90
			Inverness	(npsv)	9/90	by 4/93
7750001	E122WUA	825823	Ripon	Ripon-Masham	6/88	12/93
7750002	F911EUS	828227	Luing	Isle of Luing	9/88	6/93
			Glasgow-186	crewbus	7/93	
7770001	E794UDW	331556	Abergavenny-13	mailvan		
			Taffs Well	workshop recovery vehicle		by 1/94
7770002	E535CLG	330506	Llangollen 41 to L6	mailvan		
7770003	E536CLG	330531	Llangollen-42	mailvan		
			Wrexham-W42	mailvan		
			Macclesfield 29	mailvan		by 5/97
7770004	E537CLG	330534	Llangollen-43	mailvan		
			York	workshop recovery van	by 5/93	by 11/97
7770005	E967BJA	331175	Dobcross 37	mailvan	6/88	2/94
7770006	E968BJA	331179	Dobcross 36	mailvan	6/88	by 3/95
7770007	E969BJA	331183	Bacup RD28	mailvan	6/88	
7770008	E479KYL	331208	Postal Headquarters	Swiftair racing team (support vehicle)		
			Stanhope-SE3	mailvan		
			Darlington	mailvan reserve		by 2/97
7770009	E839RFL	331211	Swaffham-111	mailvan		
7770010	E840RFL	331298	King's Lynn-R20	mailvan reserve	7/88	by 1/97
			Downham Market	mailvan	7/88	
			King's Lynn-R4	mailvan reserve	7/88	
			Swaffham-SW111	mailvan		current
7770011	E774LPV	330593	Saxmundham	mailvan	7/88	
			Leiston-LE4	mailvan		current
			Bury St. Edmunds	mailvan		
7770012	E976CHH	330597	Tebay (TY1)	mailvan	7/88	
			Penrith (P11)	mailvan		by 12/93
7770013	F803ATH	330622	Carmarthen	workshop recovery van	9/88	current
7770014	F608SDF	333303	Hereford	workshop recovery van	1/89	current
7770015	E508FFR	330625	Burnley R7 to 5045	mailvan		by 5/97
7770016	E509FFR	331219	Rossendale	mailvan		by -/96
7770017	E501FFR	331223	Burnley 7 to 5043	mailvan		by 5/97
7770018	E499FFR	331227	Burnley 20 to 5044	mailvan		by 8/96

This standard Ford Escort hatchback, E418KTS (7720099) operated the Dollar to Glendevon service in 1991. It carried a prominent sticker in the windscreen identifying its use when photographed in Glendevon in September. A similar vehicle operated at Birnam and both routes became Land Rover operated in March 1992. *P. Walton*

7100019	E402BYS	331252	Bunessan (later BUN2)	mailvan	7/88	4/98
7100020	E403BYS	331255	Craignure	mailvan	7/88	4/98
7100021	F925EUS	331263	Glasgow-PE26	postal engineering	8/88	
			Lanark-LVM	workshop recovery van		current
7770022	F471OHT	331267	PRO South West	hot-air balloon team support	11/88	
			Dorchester-M11	workshop vehicle		
7770023	E113FSA	331270	Huntly	Huntly-Cabrach	6/88	
			Huntly-R11	reserve	12/92	10/93
7770024	E114FSA	331295	Aberdeen-R7	reserve	6/88	9/93

1988

Only four postbuses were bought, all Ford Sierra diesel estate cars, the first three arriving in August and September 1988 while the last was intended as an ordinary car and delivered in May 1989. Another car, a Peugeot 309, was utilised as an expedient Post Bus in 1990. Freight Rover recalled Sherpas for modification under warranty towards the end of 1988 and loaned the Post Office a beige Sherpa registered E55SOG with 16 coach seats. Having neither mail pen nor PSV-licence it was used as Galashiels reserve, releasing one vehicle at a time to be sent by rail from Livingston railhead to Bordesley depôt in Birmingham for treatment at the Washwood Heath factory. In contrast with the lack of new Post Buses, one hundred and sixty six assorted Sherpas were supplied as crewbuses to take staff to the large Automated Processing Centres and also from delivery offices to the start of their rounds, it no longer being acceptable for them to travel in the backs of vans.

8730070-8730119   Peugeot 309GLD saloon
8760001-8760004   Ford Sierra 2.3 diesel 4-seat estate car postbus

serial	registration	chassis no.	location	route	in	out
8730096	F161LSU	AD9202870870	Glasgow	(npsv)	7/89	
			Biggar	Biggar-Abington	c8/90	
			Glasgow-F6	(npsv)		
			Larkhall (Streamline)	(npsv)	by 3/95	
			Aberdeen	(npsv)	2/96	5/96
8760001	F106NST	JK57096	Gairloch	Gairloch-Redpoint	9/88	
			Kyle of Lochalsh	reserve	5/91	8/93
8760002	F121NST	JK68759	Canisbay	Canisbay-Wick	1/89	3/93
8760003	F122NST	JC43927	Newtonmore	Newtonmore-Kinlochlaggan	11/88	3/93
8760004	F651KKJ	JY84573	Canterbury-403	Canterbury-Grove	6/89	7/92

Four Sierra estates were ordered in 1988, three of which entered service in Scotland. The remaining one, F651KKJ (8760004), originally intended to be a car for staff use, was used to launch the Canterbury-Grove route in June 1989 carrying a hybrid livery, stating that it is a Postal Bus.
D A Cott

1989

By 1989 the Freight-Rover operation had been bought by the Dutch owned DAF company and the Sherpa name had been dropped, the facelifted range being badged Leyland-DAF. The solitary large bus purchased this year was a twin-wheel low-roof 400 14-seater at the request of North Yorkshire County Council. There is no special significance in the high serial - it was intended to avoid clashing with surviving Dodges from the 1979 delivery, the Transit whose serial it does duplicate having long gone. It was prepared at Bamber Bridge and registered for use one day only on the Cockley Beck service which appeared on the BBC Television programme 'Jim'll Fix It Christmas Special' shown in December 1989.

Two Land Rovers from the year's order for twenty-four mailvans were converted to postbuses (the first at least was treated at Bamber Bridge) but were not re-coded, while a Ford Sierra estate car was purchased locally by Scotland and an Austin Montego estate for the North East as replacements. Nine Ford Escort hatchbacks in a darker shade of red from an order for 119 cars were converted to postbuses; six were allocated to the Dumfries area of Scotland, then under the control of Carlisle District, hence the English registrations. 9730218 entered service devoid of lettering or external serials and carried a vinyl sticker in the windscreen declaring it to be 'Working for the Royal Mail', and at least one was later repainted into the correct colour.

Finally, a Peugeot 505 7-seat estate car based in Edinburgh was used on the two Inverness services for a few days in October 1988, although fairly common at the time as a taxi and 'people mover' its purchase price was more than that of a Sherpa.

serial		
9100101-9100124	Land Rover 90 60cf. mailvan	
9730186-9730304	Ford Escort 1.8DL 5-door diesel hatchback car	
9750105	Leyland-DAF Sherpa 400 14-seat postbus (Bamber Bridge conversion)	
9760001	Peugeot 505 7-seat estate car postbus	
9760002	Ford Sierra 2.3L diesel 4-seat estate car postbus	
9760003	Austin Montego 2.0 4-seat estate car postbus	

serial	registration	chassis no.	location	route	in	out
9100103	H397YAS	FA438770	Halkirk	Halkirk-Altnabreac	8/90	
			Thurso	reserve	12/92	7/98
9100116	G470UHS	FA439127	Brodick-BK5	Brodick-Pirnmill	6/90	current
9730218	G120JSC	LT68727	Kinross (K7)	Kinross-Rumbling Bridge	7/90	3/93
9730240	H359YGG	70254	Biggar	Biggar-Crawfordjohn	8/90	4/96

Opposite, top:- **A number of Postbus routes in Dumfries & Galloway were operated by Escort cars. Although part of Scotland, the area came under the control of Carlisle District at the time, so the vehicles received Carlisle index marks. Typical of these is G881PAO (9730264) pictured pausing at Penwhirn Reservoir in August 1995 on the route from Glen Luce.** *D A Cott*

Opposite, bottom:- **Four Montego estate Postbuses were bought locally by N.E.P.R. for services in the North East of England in 1985, one of which was replaced after a short life by G380YHP (9760003), which is pictured at its Alnwick base in August 1990.** *D A Cott*

9730260	G877PAO	70286	Lockerbie-(PBR3)	reserve	7/90	4/96
9730261	G878PAO	70287	Annan	Annan-Creca	7/90	4/96
9730262	G879PAO	70288	Castle Douglas-9	Castle Douglas-Corsock	7/90	4/96
9730263	G880PAO	70289	Lockerbie-1	Lockerbie-Corrie Common	7/90	4/96
9730264	G881PAO	70290	Glenluce	Glenluce-New Luce	7/90	4/98
9730265	G435PRM	70291	Lockerbie-3	Lockerbie-Waterbeck	7/90	4/96
9730266	G436PRM	70292	Lockerbie-2	Lockerbie-Hightae	7/90	4/96
9750105	G290JBV	863745	Leyburn-LN14	Leyburn-Hawes	3/90	4/94
			Northallerton-NN36	Northallerton-Hawes	4/94	3/95
9760001	E585MAC	3119087	Edinburgh	(npsv)		
			Inverness	Inverness services	10/88	10/88
			Birmingham	(npsv)		by 9/92
9760002	G340UES	LY43909	Blairgowrie-P84	Blairgowrie-Glenisla	6/90	3/92
			Perth-PL6	Distribution Manager (npsv)	9/92	by 9/97
9760003	G380YHP		Alnwick-19	Alnwick-Alnham	4/90	
			Wooler	Wooler-Donnington	6/91	3/94
			Alnwick	Alnwick-Canonburn		
			Prudhoe	(npsv)	by 1/95	by 5/96

Leyland-DAF Sherpa 400 postbus G290JBV (9750105) at Hawes on the service to Leyburn in August 1990. Note the twin rear wheels
D A Cott

Land Rovers are used as both postbuses and workshop/recovery vehicles, particularly in more remote areas. H397YAS (9100103) was originally the Halkirk to Altnabreac Postbus, but on replacement became its reserve based at Thurso workshop, where it was photographed in August 1994.
D A Cott

1990

Large buses were purchased in quantity for the first time in four years, mainly from Leyland-DAF with ten 200 10-seaters converted at Bamber Bridge being the first use of the narrow-bodied model. To comply with Certificate of Fitness requirements the front passenger seat was left in place (despite it being within the mail pen) to avoid the requirement for the first row of three seats behind to be fitted with seat belts. Eight assorted low-roof 400 models included four 16-seaters to replace Transits from 1983 and 1984. Some Sherpas were delayed in entering service due to fitting electric steps before delivery. A new Leyland-DAF 200 crewbus to replace the Talbot Express was lettered 'Royal Mail Tour Bus - Serving the Arts since 1987' and 'Delivering the Arts to Scottish Communities' and was numbered in this series, however a Leyland-DAF 400 with luxurious conversion by Crystals for YTS work at Milton Keynes was renumbered from 0750097 to 0780078 before delivery. A change was made to the Laide to Achnasheen route when the pair of Transits came up for replacement in that a single Leyland-DAF 400 bus was provided for the passengers while a Sherpa van was provided for the mail and goods traffic.

A solitary Vauxhall Midi long-wheel-base 11-seater was purchased for Penrith and it made history after replacement in 1994 with a respectable 88,000 miles on the clock when it was hired to Stagecoach subsidiary Cumberland Motor Services for six weeks under arrangements made by Cumbria County Council for service between Carlisle and Brampton. All the larger buses were numbered above the serials of the 1980 deliveries. Estate car purchases consisted of seventeen petrol and one diesel Ford Sierras followed by fifteen Peugeot diesel 405s heralding a change of policy. A Peugeot 309 car was converted to a postbus after staff use in Glasgow, while four Land Rover mailvans became postbuses but retained their original serial numbers.

0100039-0100083	Land Rover Defender 90 diesel 60cf. mailvan (♣ 4–seat postbus)
0730427-0730471	Peugeot 309GLD 1.9 4-seat saloon
0750095-0750096	Leyland-DAF Sherpa 400 14-seat postbus (Bamber Bridge conversion)
0750097	Leyland-DAF Sherpa 400 16-seat minibus (Crystals Conversions)
0750098	Leyland-DAF Sherpa 400 12-seat postbus
0750099	Leyland-DAF Sherpa 400 13-seat postbus
0750100	Leyland-DAF Sherpa 200 12-seat personnel carrier
0750101	Leyland-DAF Sherpa 200 10-seat postbus
0750102	Bedford Midi 14-seat postbus
0750103-0750111	Leyland-DAF Sherpa 200 10-seat postbus (Bamber Bridge conversion)
0750112-0750115	Leyland-DAF Sherpa 400 16-seat postbus (Bamber Bridge conversion)
0760001-0760017	Ford Sierra 1.8LX Turbo 4-seat estate car postbus
0760018	Ford Sierra 1.8 diesel 4-seat estate car postbus
0760019-0760033	Peugeot 405GLD 1.9 4-seat estate car postbus

G470DOO, a Leyland-DAF Sherpa 400 with Crystals Conversions 16-seat minibus conversion was ordered as 0750097 though it entered service with crewbus serial 0750078 as a YTS minibus at Chelmsford. *C M Hogan*

serial	registration	chassis no.	location	route	in	out
0100072♣	J463GDS	HA701869	Colonsay	Isle of Colonsay	8/91	current
0100081♣	H657CST	HA702183	Dalwhinnie	Dalwhinnie-Drummin	6/91	
			Invergarry	Invergarry-Kinlochourn	11/92	
			Fort William	reserve	5/98	current
0100082♣	H658CST	HA702290	Drumnadrochit	Drumnadrochit-Grotaig	6/91	current
0100083♣	H174DAS	HA702291	Dingwall	reserve	7/91	current
0730442	H672CDS	210386534	Glasgow-129	(npsv)	4/91	
			Balfron	Balfron-Fintry	c7/96	3/97
			Glasgow-F26		by 8/97	6/98
0750095	G394VST	872343	Laide	Laide-Achnasheen	5/90	
			Perth-R11	reserve	1/93	
			Edinburgh-R1	reserve crewbus	by 8/95	7/96
0750096	G395VST	872625	Elgol	Elgol-Broadford	7/90	
			Kyle of Lochalsh	reserve	9/91	
			Castlebay	Castlebay-Eoligarry	2/92	3/96
0780078	G470DOO	862190	Chelmsford-995	YTS minibus (npsv)	4/90	10/98
0750098	H828XSL	877410	Killin	Killin-Callander	6/90	
			Perth-PR10	reserve	3/92	9/96

Opposite, top:- **The northern corners of the Isle of Skye are both linked to Dunvegan by Postbus routes. H383YAS (0760008) is seen in August 1994, climbing back to the road from an address overlooking Loch Bay, bound for Waternish. Royal Mail vehicles in Gaelic speaking areas have bilingual lettering.** *D A Cott*
Opposite, bottom:- **There are only three ferries a week bringing mail from Oban to the Isle of Colonsay. The Land Rover Postbus undertakes a circular delivery tour of the island before wading to the neighbouring island of Oronsay at the next available low tide. J436GDS (0100072), whose predecessor was withdrawn with chassis rot after 26,000 miles, is seen arriving on Oronsay, through a rock cutting, off the beach in August 1995.** *D A Cott*

0750099	H831XSL	877469	Pitlochry-PY19	Pitlochry-Rannoch	7/90	7/97
			Kittybrewster-A42	crewbus		current
0750100	H127LSX	880455	Edinburgh	crewbus	8/90	by 8/98
0750101	H848XSL	874840	Denny-FK24	Denny-Fintry	8/90	
			Grangemouth	reserve	by 5/92	7/97
0750102	H387SET		Penrith-P6	Penrith-Martindale	11/90	7/94
			Burnley	crewebus	10/94	
			Preston		by 6/95	by 6/96
0750103	J543FSU	896756	Portnahaven	Portnahaven-Port Ellen	8/91	
			Port Ellen	reserve	2/92	8/96
0750104	J544FSU	896772	Biggar-BG10	Biggar-Tweedsmuir	11/91	6/97
			Lanark	crewbus	by 8/97	
0750105	J545FSU	896819	Larkhall	Strathaven-Dungavel	11/91	6/97
			Hamilton	crewbus	7/97	10/97
0750106	J25ECA	896929	Chester-C48	Chester-Tattenhall	9/91	7/97
0750107	J546FSU	896888	Islay	Port Askaig-Port Ellen	11/91	6/97
			Port Ellen		by 8/97	8/97
0750108	J547FSU	896901	Tiree	Isle of Tiree	8/91	8/96
0750109	J548FSU	896938	Inveraray	Inveraray-Dalmally	8/91	10/97
			Oban	reserve	by 8/94	10/96
0750110	J549FSU	896965	Bowmore-PT11	Bowmore-Port Askaig	9/91	6/96
			Port Ellen	reserve	by 2/97	10/97
0750111	J550FSU	897417	Biggar-BG12	Biggar-Newbigging	11/91	7/97
0750112	J306EST	897638	Kyle of Lochalsh	reserve	8/91	
			Elgol	Elgol-Broadford	9/91	6/97
0750113	J282EST	897727	Timsgarry	Timsgarry-Stornoway	8/91	6/96
0750114	J305EST	897835	Talmine	Talmine-Tongue-Lairg	8/91	7/97
0750115	J450GDS	901252	Dunoon-348	Dunoon-Tighnabruaich	9/91	6/97
			Larkhall-403	crewbus	6/97	9/97
0760001	H399YAS	GBBNLJ25678	Skerray	Skerray-Tongue	8/90	4/96
0760002	H401YAS	GBBNLJ26579	Lochinver	Lochinver-Drumbeg	8/90	4/96
0760003	H392YAS	GBBNLJ26580	Sanday	Sanday-Broughton	8/90	4/96
0760004	H393YAS	GBBNLJ26581	Sanday	Lady-Sanday	8/90	4/96
0760005	H394YAS	GBBNLJ26582	Kyle of Lochalsh	Kyle-Stromeferry	8/90	4/96
0760006	H402YAS	GBBNLJ26583	Kyle of Lochalsh	Kyle-Letterfearn	8/90	4/96
0760007	H395YAS	GBBNLJ26584	Lairg	Lairg-Altass	8/90	4/96
0760008	H383YAS	GBBNLJ26585	Dunvegan	Dunvegan-Waternish	8/90	4/96
0760009	H403YAS	GBBNLJ26586	Kyle of Lochalsh	Kyle-Arnisdale	8/90	4/96
0760010	H404YAS	GBBNLJ26587	Melvich	Melvich-Armadale	8/90	4/96
0760011	H406YAS	GBBNLJ26588	Dingwall	Dingwall-Heights of Dochcarty	8/90	4/96
0760012	H396YAS	GBBNLJ26589	Dunvegan	Dunvegan-Glendale	8/90	4/96
0760013	H409YAS	GBBNLJ26590	Strathconon	Strathconon-Muir of Ord	9/90	4/96
0760014	H410YAS	GBBNLJ26591	Inverness	Inverness-Gorthleck	9/90	4/96
0760015	H407YAS	GBBNLJ26592	Shieldaig	Shieldaig-Kishorn	8/90	
			Kyle of Lochalsh	reserve	12/92	
			Poolewe	Poolewe-Cove		
			Kyle of Lochalsh	reserve		4/96
0760016	H384YAS	GBBNLJ26593	Bettyhill	Bettyhill-Kinbrace	8/90	4/96
0760017	H408YAS	GBBNLJ26594	Applecross	Applecross-Toscaig	8/90	11/95
0760018	H852XSL	GBBNLP97498	Pitlochry-PY11	Pitlochry-Dalnaspidal	11/90	
			Perth-PR15	reserve	by 9/92	9/96
0760019	H871CSU	70284581	Brodick	Brodick-Shannochie	6/91	11/94
			Oban reserve		by 8/95	7/96
0760020	H807ETY	70285720	Morpeth-23	Morpeth-Whalton	6/91	2/97
0760021	H642CST	70280808	Inverness	Inverness-Tomatin	5/91	
			Lairg	reserve	c12/92	
			Kirkwall	reserve	4/96	3/97
0760022	H870CSU	70281212	Brodick	Brodick-Kilmory	6/91	
			Brodick	Brodick-Blackwaterfoot	8/94	
			Portree	reserve	11/94	3/97
0760023	H808ETY	70279258	Alnwick-19	Alnwick-Alnham	6/91	3/96
0760024	H644CST	70284903	Bernera	Bernera-Callanish	5/91	4/96
			Bernera	mailcar	4/96	10/96
0760025	H643CST	70280411	Grantown-on-Spey	Grantown-Lochindorb	5/91	3/97
0760026	H872CSU	70285244	Brodick	Brodick-Blackwaterfoot	6/91	8/94
			Kirkintilloch	Kirkintilloch-Lennoxtown	8/94	2/96
			Helensburgh	mailcar	2/97	7/97
0760027	H645CST	70278152	Gairloch	Gairloch-Redpoint	5/91	3/97
0760028	H646CST	70278063	Poolewe	Poolewe-Cove	5/91	3/97
0760029	H647CST	70278061	Rousay	Isle of Rousay	5/91	3/97
0760030	H648SET	70285136	Kylesku	Scourie-Elphin	5/91	3/97

Unique Bedford 14-seat Midi Postbus H387SET (0750102) had a long life with Royal Mail, having been purchased following a period when it was used as a demonstrator. It is pictured at Penrith, where it served on the Martindale route for four years from November 1990. It later became a crewbus at Burnley before passing to Preston. *M J Croasdale*

0760031	H869CSU	70280678	Dalmally	Bridge of Orchy-Dalmally	6/91		5/96
0760032	J307EST	70280961	Ballachulish	Ballachulish-Glen Etive	10/91		9/96
0760033	H422CNS	70278934	Balfron-F11	Balfron-Fintry	5/91		by 7/96
			Balfron	mailcar			3/97

Postbus conversions of Sherpa minibuses were undertaken at Bamber Bridge between 1986 and 1992 and included fitting a mesh screen, fire extinguisher, first aid kit, emergency exit mechanism, lettering and obtaining a Certificate of Fitness. Seen there awaiting attention in May 1991 is 0750106, later registered J25ECA for the new route from Chester to Tattenhall.
D A Cott

1991

Orders for postbuses in 1991 consisted of sixty Leyland-DAF 200 10-seaters, twelve Leyland-DAF 400 14-seaters, followed by another 10-seater, all converted at Bamber Bridge. 1750002 was loaned to Public Relations at Edinburgh for use in an episode of 'Jim'll Fix', hence its Edinburgh registration. Several of the smaller buses were reduced to 7-seats for use in the Highlands and Western Isles, by the removal of the first row behind the driver and moving the mesh screen back to allow more space for mail. 1750034 at Kelso was experimentally fitted with a pair of child safety seats by its driver, and 1750068 had an electrically operated entrance step, later added to all Scottish and South Eastern buses - some buses in Scotland having previously been fitted with manually operated ones. The first of the larger buses was reduced to 10 seats with space for one wheelchair and fitted with a rear Ratcliff chair lift for use at Sittingbourne, the cost of the modification being shared with Kent County Council.

Estate car deliveries consisted of a further twenty-four Peugeot 405s together with an identical vehicle which had been a Peugeot demonstrator. One of the batch was fitted with a sump guard for use over rough terrain on the Peebles route. Seventeen Land Rover 90 postbuses were ordered and given high 77 serials to avoid clashing with 1981 vehicles, however eleven of the batch were allocated to mailvan duties.

1750001-1750060	Leyland-DAF Sherpa 200 10-seat postbus (Bamber Bridge conversion)
	(♦ 7-seat with additional mail compartment)
1750061	Leyland-DAF Sherpa 400 10-seat postbus (Bamber Bridge conversion)(Ratcliff chair-lift)
1750062-1750072	Leyland-DAF Sherpa 400 14-seat postbus (Bamber Bridge conversion)
1750073	Leyland-DAF Sherpa 200 10-seat postbus (Bamber Bridge conversion)
1760001-1760025	Peugeot 405GLD 1.9 4-seat estate car postbus
1770101-1770121	Land Rover 90 Defender 2.5 diesel 60cf. mailvan

serial	registration	chassis no.	location	route	in	out
1750001	J562PPA	902776	Redhill-951	Redhill-Outwood	10/91	
			Redhill	reserve	3/94	
			Gillingham-R14	reserve	6/94	11/97
1750002	J151USF	902775	Rothbury-4	Rothbury-Alwinton	10/91	
			Morpeth-R1	reserve	8/92	7/97
1750003	J563PPA	902750	Oxted-953	Oxted-Lingfield	10/91	
			Canterbury 459	Canterbury-Wootton	6/93	
			Canterbury-403	Canterbury-Grove		
			Canterbury-R146	reserve	3/94	7/97
1750004	J564PPA	902774	Reigate-952	Reigate-Leigh	10/91	
			Redhill-R13	reserve	6/96	3/97
1750005	J823VUJ	908210	Llandrindod Wells- LD19	Llandrindod Wells-Llaithddu	1/92	
			Llandrindod Wells	reserve	c12/92	7/97
1750006	J230GFV	908518	Louth L8 to GY58	Louth-Goulceby	1/92	9/95
1750007	J240GFV	908563	Cupar-CP1	Cupar-Peat Inn	1/92	6/97
1750008	J826VUJ	908640	Llanidloes-LS8	Llanidloes-Llangurig	1/92	7/97
1750009	J153USF	908610	West Calder	West Calder-Tarbrax	1/92	
			Livingston-LV21	West Calder-Tarbrax		6/97
			Leven-LE11	crewbus	by 9/97	
1750010	J414VSG	908626	Edinburgh	driver trainer	1/92	6/97
			Edinburgh SE8	crewbus		
1750011	J825VUJ	908656	Llanidloes-LS7	Llanidloes-Dylife	1/92	7/97

Due to a loss of subsidies, and poor passenger numbers, two of the routes operating from Canterbury were withdrawn in April 1997. K404 MGJ (0760017) is seen preparing to leave Canterbury Delivery Office yard for what was thought to be its penultimate afternoon run. Within the month it had been re-instated though it was finally withdrawn in April 1998. *D A Cott*

1750012	J165USF	908707	Dunbar-DB1	Dunbar-Innerwick	1/92	7/97
			Edinburgh SE9	crewbus	7/97	
1750013	J154USF	908726	Dalkeith-DAB	Gorebridge-Moorfoot	1/92	7/97
			Edinburgh	crewbus		11/97
1750014♦	J330EST	909369	Lochmaddy	Lochmaddy-Sidinish	2/92	
			Oban	reserve (upseated to 10)	8/96	7/97
1750015♦	J622FAS	908946	Alligin	Alligin-Kinlochewe	2/92	6/97
1750016♦	J621FAS	908784	Tigharry	Tigharry-Airport	3/92	
			Lochmaddy			
			Scarinish	Isle of Tiree (upseated to 10)		6/97
			Scarinish	crewbus	by 8/97	
1750017	J623FAS	908792	Dingwall	reserve	2/92	3/94
			Falkirk-FK40	crewbus	c3/94	2/98
1750018♦	J624FAS	908812	Thurso	Thurso-Wick Airport	2/92	6/97
1750019	J625FAS	908769	Lairg	reserve	2/92	8/92
			Kirriemuir F5 -K151	Kirriemuir-Glen Clova	8/92	6/97
1750020	J626FAS	908868	Dingwall	reserve	by 8/92	
			Aberfeldy-PY5	Aberfeldy-Glen Lyon	c8/93	7/97
			Leven-LE13	crewbus	by 9/97	12/97
1750021	J639FAS	908901	Castlebay	Castlebay-Eoligarry	3/92	3/96
1750022	J627FAS	908896	Stornoway	reserve	2/92	8/96
			Port Ellen	Bowmore-Port Askaig	9/96	6/97
			Glasgow	crewbus		
1750023	J636FAS	908884	Portree	reserve	3/92	
			Brodick	reserve	11/94	
			Ayr-R1	reserve	7/97	3/98
1750024♦	J638FAS	910056	Lochmaddy	Lochmaddy-Newton Sollas	2/92	
			Lochmaddy	Lochmaddy-Airport	3/92	
			Lochboisdale	reserve	8/96	
			Port Ellen	reserve		10/97
1750025	J166USF	908918	Melrose-MR7	Galashiels-Lilliesleaf	1/92	7/97
			Edinburgh area	crewbus		10/97

1750026	J203VSF	908917	Galashiels-GLR4	reserve	1/92	7/97
			Edinburgh Dell-D9	crewbus	by 11/97	2/98
1750027	J221VSF	909194	Leven-LV15	Leven-New Gilston	1/92	9/94
1750028	J841VSF	908945	Cupar-R4	reserve	3/92	
			Glenrothes-FR4	crewbus reserve	7/97	5/98
1750029	J824VUJ	908699	Aberystwyth	Aberystwyth-Cwmystwyth	1/92	7/97
1750030	J832VSF	908945	Hawick-HK16	Hawick-Bonchester Bridge	1/92	6/97
1750031	J962NKL	909834	Tun.Wells N-200	Tunbridge Wells-Mayfield	2/92	6/96
1750032	J834VSF	908973	Linlithgow-LN7	Linlithgow-Blackness	2/92	
			Aberfeldy-PY6	Aberfeldy-Killin	1/95	
			Leven-LE2	crewbus		12/97
1750033	J831VSF	908986	Haddington-HDB	Haddington-Garvald	3/92	7/97
			Edinburgh area	crewbus		12/97
1750034	J833VSF	908999	Kelso-KO2	Kelso-Stichill	1/92	6/97
			Edinburgh Dell-D1	crewbus	by 11/97	c1/98
1750035	J382HYS	909859	Port Ellen	reserve	2/92	
			Oban	reserve	2/97	11/97
1750036	J383HYS	911040	Oban	reserve	2/92	
			Lochgilphead	Lochgilphead/Inveraray-Dalmally	by 8/94	7/97
1750037	J640FAS	910968	Kyle of Lochalsh	reserve	2/92	
			Dingwall	reserve		6/97
			Edinburgh-R8	crewbus reserve	by 12/97	current
1750038	J656AAO	911007	Annan	Annan-Powfoot	2/92	
			Coatbridge-C2	crewbus	7/97	1/98
1750039	J657AAO	910499	Thornhill	Thornhill-Moniaive	2/92	
			Coatbridge-C3	crewbus	7/97	1/98
1750040	J658AAO	910674	Castle Douglas-3	Castle Douglas-Mossdale	2/92	6/97
			Rutherglen	crewbus		3/98
1750041	J659AAO	910460	Kirkcudbright	Kirkcudbright-Borgue	2/92	6/97
			Rutherglen-415	crewbus		4/98
1750042	J724NTA	911169	Honiton	Honiton-Luppitt	3/92	12/97
1750043	J79NTT	911360	Wadebridge	Wadebridge-Penrose	3/92	current
1750044	J660AAO	911469	Castle Douglas-13	Castle Douglas-Auchencairn	2/92	7/97
			Glasgow Cubie St	415 crewbus	10/97	6/98
1750045	J361NKM	911468	Canterbury-440	Canterbury-Crundale	3/92	6/96
1750046	J532PPC	911438	Petersfield-P21	Petersfield-Froxfield	3/92	7/97
1750047	J257SAN	911607	Newbury NB4R	reserve	3/92	
			Swindon-PBR	reserve	by 11/95	7/97
1750048	J663AAO	911479	Castle Douglas	reserve	2/92	
			Lockerbie-R	reserve	-/93	by 7/97
			Glasgow-SR3	crewbus reserve	12/97	7/98
1750049	J153LRN	911527	Barrow-in-Furness	reserve	2/92	
			Ulverston	Ulverston-Grizedale Forest	3/96	7/97
1750050	J154LRN	911581	Broughton-in-Furness	Broughton-Cockley Beck	2/92	7/97
1750051	J155LRN	911528	Ulverston	Ulverston-Grizedale Forest	2/92	
			Ulverston-R7	reserve	by 4/97	7/97
1750052	J258SAN	911522	Newbury N58-NB3	Newbury-Chaddleworth	3/92	7/97
1750053	J661AAO	911608	Lockerbie-3	Lockerbie-St. Ann's	1/92	7/97
			Rutherglen-417	crewbus	9/97	6/98
1750054	J673RPM	911624	Dorking 955 to 855	Dorking-Ockley	3/92	
			Maidstone	Maidstone-Coxheath		
			Dorking-855	Dorking-Ockley		6/96
1750055	J259SAN	911654	Hungerford	Lamborn-Hungerford	3/92	
			Newbury-NB4	crewbus		
			Hungerford-HB1	Lamborn-Hungerford		7/97
1750056	J260SAN	911590	Newbury N57-NB2	Newbury-West Ilsley	3/92	7/97
1750057	J662AAO	911583	Lockerbie	reserve	2/92	
			Bellshill	crewbus	9/97	3/98

Opposite, top:- **There are two routes that serve the Caithness town of Wick, one uses an estate car to John O'Groats while the other uses a larger vehicle to link Thurso to Wick airport. Sherpa J624 FAS (1750018) is pictured at the airport in August 1994 where services are timed to suit airline arrivals and departures.** *D A Cott*

Opposite, bottom:- **Many of 1992 delivery of Land Rovers were used only as mailvans. One that was used as a postbus was J479FSR (1770101) which entered service from Kirriemuir on the Glen Prosen service but it was soon sent to Perth as a reserve later moving to Dundee as reserve-R151.** *P Walton*

1750058	J674RPM	911714	Redhill-954	reserve	3/92	
			Maidstone	Maidstone-Sutton Valence	4/94	6/96
			Gillingham	reserve	6/96	current
1750059	J473FSR	911994	Dundee-F4R	reserve	3/92	
			Dundee-R152	reserve		7/97
			Dundee	crewbus	9/97	2/98
1750060	J771VFA	911744	Builth Wells-BS5	Builth Wells-Painscastle	4/92	5/98
1750061	J31LFR	909727	Sittingbourne-341	Sittingbourne-Wormshill	1/92	8/97
1750062	J472FSR	910661	Aberfeldy-PY6	Aberfeldy-Lawers/Bridgend-Kenmore	3/92	
			Linlithgow-LN7	Linlithgow-Blackness/Maddiston	1/95	
			Perth-PR11	reserve	7/95	7/97
			Dundee D117	crewebus	7/97	4/98
1750063	J590ESL	910684	Crianlarich-C22	Crianlarich-Killin	3/92	8/97
1750064	J474FSR	910706	Grangemouth-FK006	reserve	3/92	
			Denny-FK24	Denny-Fintry		7/97
			Edinburgh NW11	crewbus		
			Edinburgh-R26	crewbus reserve	6/98	current
1750065	J601ESL	910631	Aberfoyle S9 to S11	Aberfoyle-Inversnaid	3/92	8/97
			Dalkeith-DA1	crewbus	by 9/97	
			Edinburgh R1-XR1	crewbus reserve		8/98
1750066	J475FSR	910630	Killin-C21	Killin-Callander	3/92	7/97
1750067	J602ESL	910599	Kirriemuir-F5	Kirriemuir-Glen Clova	3/92	
			Lairg	Durness for Altnaharra (summer)	8/92	
			Dingwall	reserve	11/96	7/97
1750068	J477FSR	910606	Aberfeldy-PY5	Aberfeldy-Kenmore/Glen Lyon	3/92	
			Lairg	Lairg-Durness		
			Lairg	reserve	by 2/95	7/97
			Aberdeen	crewbus		3/98
1750069	J470FSR	910613	Callander-S37	Callander-Trossachs	3/92	8/97
			Inverclyde-411	crewbus		2/98
1750070	J476FSR	910756	Aberfoyle S49 to S9	Aberfoyle-Kinlochard	3/92	8/97
			Inverclyde-412	crewbus	by 10/97	2/98
1750071	J471FSR	910803	Blairgowrie-P83	Blairgowrie-Glenshee	3/92	
			Laide	Laide-Achnasheen	1/93	
			Kyle of Lochalsh	reserve		
			Dingwall	reserve	2/95	
			Laide	Laide-Achnasheen	11/96	7/97
1750072	K521FWY	915031	Morpeth-4	Morpeth-Rothbury-Alwinton	8/92	12/96
1750073	J386DUG	917265	Alnwick	Wooler-Alnwick	5/92	9/95
1760001	H836ETY	70311120	Rothbury	Rothbury-Biddlestone	7/91	2/97
1760002	J641FAS	70515728	Melvich	Melvich-Kinbrace	3/92	3/97
1760003	J961VSG	70515197	Cupar-CP4	Cupar-Brunton	3/92	4/98
1760004	J969VSG	70515829	West Linton-WL4	West Linton-Romanno Bridge	3/92	12/92
			Peebles-WL4	West Linton-Romanno Bridge	12/92	4/98
1760005	J975VSG	70636405	Cupar-CP18	Cupar-Newburgh	3/92	4/98
1760006	J979VSG	70517268	Selkirk-SK2	Selkirk-Ashkirk	5/92	2/97
1760007	J962VSG	70515840	Hawick-HK15	Hawick-Craik	3/92	3/97
1760008	J974VSG	70525276	Duns DS3 to DS12	Duns-Abbey St. Bathans/	3/92	
				Longformacus/Cranshaws		
			Selkirk	Selkirk-Ashkirk	c2/97	by 2/98
1760009	J970VSG	70516960	Anstruther-ANS2	Anstruther-Arncroach	3/92	4/98
1760010	J971VSG	70516501	Kelso-KO4	Kelso-Hassington/Smailholm	3/92	3/97
			Helensburgh		3/97	6/98
1760011	J972VSG	70515430	Kelso-KO3	Kelso-Roxburgh	3/92	10/98
1760012	K403MGJ	70515122	Canterbury	driver-trainer (probably)		
			Sittingbourne	Sittingbourne-Hartlip	5/93	
			Rochester (PB1)	Rochester-Cooling	c10/93	11/97
1760013	J642FAS	70517129	Nairn	Nairn-Glenferness	3/92	3/97
1760014	J643FAS	70515132	Invergordon	Invergordon-Kildermorie	3/92	3/97
1760015	J963VSG	70515664	Selkirk-SK2	Selkirk-Ashkirk	1/92	c5/92
			Melrose-MR4	Melrose-Maxton		
			Galashiels	reserve		4/94
1760016	J973VSG	70534851	Galashiels-GLR5	reserve	5/92	
			Peebles-PB11	Peebles-Manorhead	7/92	4/98
1760017	K404MGJ	70525933	Canterbury-458	Canterbury-Marshside	5/93	4/98
1760018	J841VUJ	70473389	Machynlleth	Machynlleth-Aberhosan	2/92	3/97
1760019	J657ASO	70481705	Banchory	Banchory-Ballater	2/92	4/96
1760020	J381HYS	70480766	Oban	reserve	2/92	
			Aros	Salen-Ulva Ferry	8/95	3/97
1760021	J756ASO	70468772	Forres-F10	Forres-Braemoray	2/92	3/97
1760022	J408HYS	70481132	Tarbert	Tarbert-Skipness	1/92	3/97

K521FWY (1750072) was one of the twelve Leyland-DAF high-roof Sherpas bought in 1991/92. It was photographed at Morpeth in 1994. *D Longbottom*

1760023	J471ASO	70481367	Huntly	Huntly-Lumsden		2/92	3/97
1760024	J133UUH	70481026	Abergavenny 10	Abergavenny-Skenfrith		5/92	5/97
1760025	H912FDU	70118853	Aboyne	Aboyne-Logie Coldstone		2/92	10/98
1770100	J478FSR	908912	Dunblane-S12	Dunblane-Braco		3/92	current
1770101	J479FSR	909095	Kirriemuir-F6	Kirriemuir-Glen Prosen		3/92	
			Perth	reserve		1/93	
			Dundee-R151	reserve		by 2/95	current
1770102	J480FSR	909117	Alloa S13 to AL13	Dollar-Glendevon		3/92	current
1770103	J481FSR	909068	Pitlochry PY11	Pitlochry-Dalnaspidal		3/92	
			Dingwall	reserve		2/97	current
1770104	J482FSR	909070	Birnam-PY10	Birnam-Aberfeldy		3/92	current
1770105	J483FSR	909120	Blairgowrie-P84	Blairgowrie-Glenisla		3/92	current
1770106	J281RNF	908906	Todmorden-TODLR2	mailvan		3/92	current
1770107	J282RNF	909045	Bacup-BACLR2	mailvan		3/92	current
1770108	J649FAS	911993	Inverness	mailvan		3/92	current
1770109	J650FAS	911614	Inverness	mailvan		3/92	current
1770110	J641GAS	911580	Drumnadrochit	mailvan		3/92	current
1770111	J642GAS	911590	Glenfinnan	mailvan (kept at Polloch)		3/92	current
1770112	J643GAS	911575	Balivanich	mailvan		3/92	current
1770113	J489FSR	911684	Perth-P12R	mailvan		3/92	
			Edinburgh Airport	mailvan		by 6/94	
			Perth	mailvan		by 8/95	
			Dundee-R175	mailvan			
			Girvan-G8	mailvan		2/97	current
1770114	J702FTS	911658	Pitlochry-PY15	mailvan		3/92	current
1770115	J703FTS	911659	Pitlochry-PY17	mailvan		3/92	current
1770116	J704FTS	911660	Pitlochry-PY18	mailvan		3/92	current
1770117	WXI4595	911606	Belfast-28	mailvan		3/92	current
1770118	WXI4596	911607	Omagh	mailvan		3/92	current
1770119	J225VEF	911581	Bishop Auckland-BA31	mailvan		3/92	current
1770120	J420DUG	911661	Bradford West-BDW	mailvan		3/92	current
1770121	J536WBF	911610	Colne-5307	mailvan		3/92	5/97

1992

Orders in 1992 consisted of 41 assorted Leyland-DAF's, thirty-two 200 models in three batches, three being 8-seaters for the Chippenham routes having the inward-facing nearside pair replaced by a mail pen and the remainder being conventional 10-seaters. 2750018 featured recommendations of DiPTAC (Disabled Persons Transport Advisory Committee) including brightly coloured handrails to assist the visually impaired and an electrically operated entrance step. The rest of the delivery was 400s, one downseated to 10 with a second mesh screen behind the nearside loading door, the resulting compartment being used solely for mail on the run between Enniskillen and Belfast Airport, one with 10 seats plus mail stowage for Lochmaddy airport, three with 14-seats, one with 15-seats and four with 16-seats. The first sixteen were converted at Bamber Bridge, the rest at the replacement Transport Engineering Centre at Chorley. Delivery commenced in August 1992 but allocation was again protracted as new routes were inaugurated and the last being registered in September 1994. 2750032 was registered by London Division for use as an escort on an Aid for Romania mission of four mailvans. 2750014/5 initially alternated between the Fairseat and Betsham services on a weekly basis. 2750039 was displayed at the Glasgow Transport Museum on the occasion of the 25th Anniversary of Scottish postbuses on 10th September 1993.

Fifteen Peugeot 405 estate cars were delivered in three batches, eight in June 1992, six early in 1993 and the last a local purchase in July, most replacing Sierras from 1986-88 but a number commenced new services. 2760013/5 were originally delivered to Scotland and were allocated registrations K425 BSG and K427 BSG.

Fifteen Land Rover Defender 90 postbuses were delivered and four of the contemporary mailvans were chosen for conversion to dual-purpose reserves with Scottish Mail Bus lettering and four seats in the loadspace, one also receiving a roof beacon and spotlight as a workshop recovery vehicle at Grangemouth, however another of the four was not required in Scotland and eventually found use as the workshop van at Guildford. In a new departure two Land Rover Defender 110 station wagons downseated to 8 were purchased for services carrying exceptional goods traffic over difficult terrain, together with a single 110 van also with 8-seats which was later fitted with side windows. The Blairgowrie station wagon was loaned to a school in Peebles for two months in the summer of 1995 for a trip to Iceland. 2770032 was fitted with side-windows by August 1997.

Routes from Blairgowrie and Kirriemuir have an allocation of a Land Rover 110 8-seat station wagon. K408BSG (2770015) is seen loading at Bridge of Cally Post Office in August 1993 prior to continuing the route up Glenshee, where it delivers provisions and papers in addition to the mail. *D A Cott*

2100011-2100017	Land Rover Defender 90 diesel 60cf. mailvan	
2750001-2750003	Leyland-DAF Sherpa 200 10-seat postbus (Bamber Bridge conversion)(‡ 8-seats)	
2750004-2750006	Leyland-DAF Sherpa 400 14-seat postbus (Bamber Bridge conversion)	
2750007-2750015	Leyland-DAF Sherpa 200 10-seat postbus (Bamber Bridge conversion)(‡ 8-seats)	
2750016	Leyland-DAF Sherpa 400 15-seat postbus (Bamber Bridge conversion)	
2750017-2750036	Leyland-DAF Sherpa 200 10-seat postbus (Chorley conversion)	
2750037-2750041	Leyland-DAF Sherpa 400 16-seat postbus (Chorley conversion)	
	(♥10-seats with additional mail/luggage space)	
2760001-2760015	Peugeot 405GRD 4-seat postbus	
2770015-2770016	Land Rover Defender 110Tdi station wagon 8-seat postbus	
2770017-2770031	Land Rover Defender 90 4-seat postbus	
2770032	Land Rover Defender 110 4-seat postbus	

serial	registration	chassis no.	location	route	in	out
2100014	L451CPG	919763	Guildford	recovery vehicle	9/93	
			Banbury	recovery vehicle	7/98	current
2100015	K384BSG	919813	Grangemouth-FK16	reserve & workshop recovery	11/92	current
2100016	K385BSG	919872	Perth-R9	reserve	11/92	current
2100017	K386BSG	919908	Pitlochry-PY16	mailvan	11/92	current
2750001	K282BSG	921697	Edinburgh-PBR	postbus reserve	9/92	
			Dell-D10	crewbus	8/97	by 8/98
2750002	K544FWY	921752	Skipton-SK36	Skipton-Malham	10/92	8/97
2750003‡	K631WPG	922467	Chippenham-PB1	Chippenham-N Wraxall/ Lyneham	3/93	current
2750004	K242BSG	923915	Lochinver	Lochinver-Lairg	8/92	
			Aberdeen	crewbus	7/97	
2750005	K241BSG	923859	Durness	Durness-Lairg	8/92	by 8/97
2750006	XXI7400	927803	Enniskillen-(E28)	Maguiresbridge-Enniskillen	11/92	current

Shortly before reallocation to Perth as a reserve vehicle, Gaelic lettered K265 DSG (2750037) is seen outside Clachan Post Office, North Uist, returning to Lochmaddy from its morning run to Balivanich airport in August 1996. To accommodate the amount of mail received from the plane, the grille has been moved further back, with a consequent reduction in seating. *D A Cott*

2750007	K457BRE	927116	Aberystwyth	Aberystwyth-Blaenpennal	11/92	current
2750008	K698BFA	927072	Llandrindod Wells	Llandrindod Wells-Llaithddu	11/92	4/98
			Llandrindod Wells	reserve	4/98	current
2750009	K489BRE	927039	Newtown-NE25R	reserve	11/92	current
2750010	K703BFA	927251	Newtown-NE24	Newtown-New Mills	11/92	current
2750011	K699BFA	927023	Builth Wells-BS12	Builth Wells-Abergwesyn	11/92	current
2750012‡	K632WPG	927184	Chippenham-PB2	Chippenham-Lyneham/Sopworth	3/93	current
2750013‡	K633WPG	932516	Chippenham-PB3	Chippenham-Sopworth and Melksham		
				/Reading	3/93	10/98
2750014	K401MGJ	932446	Gravesend-GL25	Gravesend-Fairseat	5/93	8/97
2750015	K406MGJ	932409	Gravesend-GL26	Gravesend-Betsham	5/93	8/97
2750016	K856CEH	933175	Llandrindod Wells LD1	Llandrindod Wells-Rhayader	2/93	current
2750017	K334NGT	932653	Canterbury-460	Canterbury-Westmarsh	5/93	12/93
			Canterbury-478	reserve		
			Haywards Heath-321	Haywards Heath-Balcombe	3/95	
			Redhill-RHR14	reserve	5/96	current
2750018	K655EEH	932533	Welshpool WL-WL21	Welshpool-Foel	7/93	current
2750019	K985BUK	932375	Stafford-402	Stafford-Eccleshall	6/93	current
2750020	K335NGT	932532	Maidstone-22	Maidstone-Stockbury Village	5/93	
			Maidstone (24)	M-Lenham Heath/Sutton Valence		
			Maidstone-22	Maidstone-Stockett Lane	10/97	current
2750021	L711JFA	932551	Middlewich 51 to 29	Middlewich-Crewe	9/93	current
2750022	K511WTT	932642	Llandovery-LDY7	Llandovery-Myddfai	7/93	current
2750023	K297AOL	932672	Stafford-400	Stafford-Knighton	6/93	current
2750024	L707VGN	932741	Canterbury	reserve	12/93	
			Canterbury 459	Canterbury-Wootton	3/94	
			Canterbury R146	reserve, later crewbus	7/97	current
2750025	L349HOL	932710	Rugeley-RUPB1	Rugeley-Abbots Bromley	6/94	current

Some postbuses are used for other purposes prior to entering service, and gain 'out of area' index marks in the process. L128VEG (2750031) was registered by Royal Mail Anglia for publicity work before its use at Pembroke Dock, while sister K630EYX (2750032) was registered in London for a humanitarian trip to Slovenia before commencing work on the Stafford to Eccleshall route, where it was photographed in August 1998. *D A Cott*

2750026	K446BSG	933311	Grangemouth-FK32	reserve	6/93	
			Grangemouth-R25	reserve		
			Cowdenbeath	crewbus	8/97	current
2750027	L421RWY	932864	Newcastle-122	crewbus	7/94	
			Gateshead-GR6	crewbus reserve	by 8/98	current
2750028	M979HDV	932903	Pembroke Dock-P18	Pembroke Dock-Bosherston	10/94	current
2750029	M980HDV	933010	Narberth N4 to N1	Narberth-Landshipping	10/94	current
2750030	L48GOK	932935	Stoke-on-Trent 403	Leek-Wetton	7/94	current
2750031	L128VEG	932986	RM Anglia Division	publicity use	7/94	
			Pembroke Dock-P16	Pembroke Dock-Angle	10/94	current
2750032	K630EYX	932925	RM London	used on trip to Slovenia	5/93	
			Stafford-401	Stafford-Eccleshall	6/93	current
2750033	M981 HDV	933038	Narberth-N3	Narberth-Lawrenny	10/94	
			Brecon (BN12)	Brecon-Talgarth	4/97	7/97
			Honiton	Honiton-Luppitt	12/97	current
2750034	K336NGT	933020	Maidstone-24	Maidstone-Lenham Heath	5/93	
			Maidstone-24	Maidstone-Stockbury Village		
			Maidstone-R14	reserve	6/98	current
2750035	M487TBF	933070	Aberystwyth	Aberystwyth-Cwmerfyn	9/94	current
2750036	K303AOL	933104	Stafford	reserve	6/93	
			Lutterworth-PB1	Lutterworth-Peatling Parva	10/93	10/96
			Rugby	stored		
			Stoke-R7	reserve	6/98	current
2750037♥	K265DSG	933077	Lochmaddy	Lochmaddy-Airport/Balivanich	6/93	
			Perth-PR10	reserve as 16-seater		
			Dundee Central	crewbus	8/97	current
2750038	L708VGN	932966	Redhill	Redhill-Outwood	3/94	12/97
2750039	K275DSG	933209	Luing	Isle of Luing	6/93	5/95
			Dunoon	Dunoon-Tighnabruaich	5/95	7/97
2750040	L594ONW	933080	Ripon-RP	Ripon-Masham	12/93	current
2750041	L748OGX	933157	Ashford A403 to 903	Ashford-Biddenden	6/94	12/97

Each workshop has a reserve pool to cover vehicles off the road. Perth has three Postbus reserves, one of which is dual purpose Land Rover K385 BSG (2100016), lettered as a Postbus but also available for other Land Rover work. It is seen outside Aberfeldy Post Office in August 1993. The other two reserves at Perth are both LDV Convoys. *D A Cott*

The Ballater to Linn of Dee route sees a lot of seasonal use to and from the Glenshee ski-lift, and has Land Rover 110 8-seater K392BSG (2770032) allocated. *D A Cott*

2760001	J820GGJ	70609877	Canterbury-403	Canterbury-Grove	7/92	
			Oxted-953	Oxted-Lingfield	6/93	2/97
2760002	K405MGJ	70650595	Canterbury-459	Canterbury-Wootton	5/93	
			Canterbury-403	Canterbury-Grove	6/93	4/98
2760003	K402MGJ	70642852	Rochester	Rochester-Cooling	5/93	
			Sittingbourne	Sittingbourne-Hartlip	by 10/93	
			Sittingbourne	reserve		current
2760004	J902WFS	70545640	Bressay	Isle of Bressay	7/92	10/98
2760005	J978WFS	70547183	Galashiels-GLR5	reserve	7/92	6/93
2760006	J979WFS	70567022	Cupar-CP5	Cupar-Birkhill	7/92	6/98
2760007	K253BSG	70548848	Fort William	Fort William-Glen Etive	11/92	10/98
2760008	J48XSC	70550362	Scourie	Scourie-Kylestrome	7/92	
			Lairg	reserve	4/96	current
2760009	K421BSG	70919154	Lairg	reserve	2/93	
			Melrose	Melrose-Maxton	4/94	11/94
			Galashiels-GLR5	reserve	by 1/95	current
2760010	K422BSG	70918062	John O'Groats	Canisbay-Wick	3/93	current
2760011	K423BSG	70915769	Shieldaig	Shieldaig-Kishorn	2/93	
			Kyle of Lochalsh	reserve	4/96	current
2760012	K424BSG	70916114	Newtonmore	Newtonmore-Kinlochlaggan	3/93	10/98
2760013	K343NGT	70916909	Maidstone	M-Coxheath/Sutton Valence	5/93	4/94
			Horsham	Horsham-Maplehurst	5/94	5/98
			Horsham	car (npsv)	5/98	10/98
2760014	K426BSG	70912399	Kinross-K7	Kinross-Rumbling Bridge	3/93	10/98
2760015	K647EEH	70919263	Alston	Alston-Brampton	7/93	6/95
			Machynlleth-R	reserve	by 7/96	11/98
2770015	K408BSG	919731	Blairgowrie-P83	Blairgowrie-Glenshee	1/93	current
2770016	K409BSG	919737	Kirriemuir F1-K152	Kirriemuir-Glen Prosen	1/93	current
2770017	K390BSG	919863	Huntly	Huntly-Clatt	11/92	current
2770018	K391BSG	919720	Huntly	Huntly-Cabrach	11/92	
			Huntly	reserve		
			Aberdeen	reserve		
			Elgin-R7	reserve	by 8/97	current
2770019	L907JSF	919863	Huntly	reserve	9/93	
			Huntly	Huntly-Cabrach		current
2770020	L908JSF	919807	Aberdeen-R7	reserve	9/93	current
2770021	K255BSG	919762	Fort William	reserve	11/92	
			Invergarry	Invergarry-Kinlochourn	1/98	current
2770022	K261BSG	919778	Rogart	Lairg-Rogart	11/92	current
2770023	K256BSG	919765	Kyle of Lochalsh	dual-purpose reserve	11/92	
			Lairg	reserve	by 8/97	
			Dingwall	reserve		current
2770024	K257BSG	919791	Dalwhinnie	Dalwhinnie-Drummin	11/92	current
2770025	K254BSG	919792	Dingwall	reserve	12/92	2/97
2770026	K258BSG	919787	Ardgay	Ardgay-Strathoykel	11/92	current
2770027	K259BSG	919860	Durness	Durness-Lairg via Altnaharra	11/92	
			Lairg	reserve		
			Thurso	reserve	by 8/97	current
2770028	K279BSG	919861	Rogart	Rogart-Scibercross	12/92	current
2770029	K331BSG	919915	Ardgay	Ardgay-Craigs	12/92	current
2770030	K262BSG	919930	Halkirk	Halkirk-Altnabreac	11/92	current
2770031	K263BSG	919870	Tomatin	Tomatin-Inverness	11/92	current
2770032	K392BSG	920184	Ballater	Ballater-Linn of Dee	11/92	current

L451CPG (2100014) was intended for use as a postbus in Scotland but was instead sent to Guildford and became a workshop van. It is pictured here in August 1994 returning an electric tractor to Guildford station. Note how it retained its Scottish livery. *PJ Rogers*

Rogart Post Office is the home of two Land Rover Postbuses, which share the routes to Sciberscross and West Langwell & Lairg to balance up their mileages. K279 BSG (2770028) awaits its next duty there in August 1993. *D A Cott*

1993

At the beginning of 1993 the Dutch owner of Leyland-DAF failed, however a management buy-out in April saved the van factory, which again provided the majority of buses with nine of the 10-seat 200s, seven 400 15-seaters and a single 400 11-seater with a Mirage wheelchair lift.

The highlight of the year was a long-awaited purpose-built bus for the busy Laide to Achnasheen service. An Iveco-Ford Turbo Daily chassis arrived from Italy in mid 1994 and by the end of the year had been bodied by Mellor Coachcraft at Rochdale following completion of a large order for Transit Holdings. It featured a modified version of their standard product having 16-seats and a large mail compartment at the rear, and incorporated most of the DiPTAC recommendations including a driver-controlled entry door. It was withdrawn in October 1996 and stood forlorn in Lairg workshop yard until being sold at British Car Auctions in Manchester in June 1997 to Selwyn Travel of Runcorn, among other duties it is used in a white livery to ferry aircrews from Manchester Airport to nearby hotels.

Five more Peugeot 405 estate cars, were purchased, two locally and three diverted from other duties retaining their 73 type codes; 3760002 had a sliding/rotating passenger seat to allow easier access for a disabled passenger. A Peugeot 306 from a large batch of general-purpose cars, 3730570, stood in at Balfron in August 1997.

Peugeot 306 saloon L291MFS (3730570) was a stand-in at Balfron, seen here in August 1997. *P D Robinson*

Illustrating the Mirage wheelchair tail-lift fitted to L494TAV (3750018) used by Royal Mail Anglia at Saffron Walden is this photograph taken at a Royal Mail 'Funday' at Duxford in September 1995. *C M Hogan*

Many 1993 LDV postbuses were only used as crewbuses including M24LYV (3750009) which, despite its postbus lettering, has only ever been used as an non-pcv with the PRO in Scotland. It is pictured at the new Edinburgh workshop in August 1998. *C M Hogan*

3730250-3730258	Peugeot 405GLD 1.9 estate car (♠ 4-seat postbus)
3730443-3730608	Peugeot 306XLD 1.9 saloon
3750001-3750013	Leyland-DAF Sherpa 200 10-seat postbus (Chorley conversion)
3750014	Iveco Turbo Daily 59.12 16-seat postbus (Mellor bodywork with mail compartment)
3750015	Leyland-DAF Sherpa 200 12-seat postbus (Chorley conversion)
3750016	Leyland-DAF Sherpa 400 15-seat postbus (Chorley conversion)
3750017	Leyland-DAF Sherpa 200 10-seat postbus (Chorley conversion)
3750018	Leyland-DAF Sherpa 400 11-seat postbus (Mirage chair-lift - Chorley conversion)
3760001-3760002	Peugeot 405GLD 1.9 4-seat estate car postbus

serial	registration	chassis no.	location	route	in	out
3730255♠	L377LFA	71154720	Carlisle	reserve	1/94	current
3730256♠	L523LSX	71154838	Dingwall	reserve	3/94	8/97
3730257♠	L274PNW	71154300	Alnwick-31	Alnwick-Wooler	3/94	5/98
3730570	L291MFS		Glasgow	(npsv)	7/94	
			Balfron	Balfron-Fintry	8/97	
			Glasgow	(npsv)		current
3750001	L37GOK	935944	Stoke-on-Trent 406	crewbus	3/94	7/98
3750002	L750PFA	935951	Penrith-P6	Penrith-Martindale	7/94	current
3750003	L38GOK	935945	Stoke-on-Trent 407	crewbus	3/94	current
3750004	M491KOL	936057	Lichfield-LF89	crewbus	9/94	
			Kingswinford-KF104	crewbus	7/98	current
3750005	M753TSF	936021	Brodick-BK9	Arran services (South)	11/94	
			Brodick-BK8	reserve	7/97	current
3750006	M754TSF	936033	Brodick-BK10	Arran services (North)	11/94	current
3750007	M21LYV	936290	Leven-LE15	Leven-New Gilston	10/94	
			Islay	Islay services	by 5/98	
			Grangemouth-R18	reserve	by 8/98	current
3750008	M23LYV	936278	Ware-WAR325	Ware-Buntingford	11/94	current
3750009	M24LYV	936286	Edinburgh-PRO1	crewbus	10/94	current
3750010	M406WEW	936900	Romford	crewbus	9/94	current
3750011	M404WEW	936880	Great Yarmouth-	crewbus	9/94	current
3750012	M985HDV	936937	Plymouth (West Park 6)	crewbus	9/94	current
3750013	M991HDV	937140	Cheltenham-1	crewbus	9/94	current
3750014	M736VSC	112537	Laide	Braemore Jct/Laide-Achnasheen	2/95	11/96
3750015	M479EDH	938905	Borrowash-241	crewbus	10/94	current
3750016	L586DPD	941162	Chippenham-CH35	crewbus	2/94	
			Northolt	stored		
			Swindon-80	crewbus	4/98	
			Hawkesworth-HW11	crewbus	by 8/98	current
3750017	M25LYV	942959	Driffield	driver-trainer	7/95	
			Alnwick	Alnwick-Wooler	9/95	
			Alnwick-R1	reserve	7/97	current
3750018	L494TAV	942672	Saffron Walden-148	Saffron Walden-U Langley	8/94	current
3760001	L720JFA	271090974	Brampton (BN5)	Brampton-Castle Carrock/Alston	1/94	10/98
3760002	L232LSC	271161222	Galashiels	reserve	1/94	
			Lismore	Isle of Lismore	6/94	10/98

Opposite, top:- **Peugeot 405 L274PNW** retained its car serial 3730257 although it undertook regular postbus on the Alnwick to Wooler service from March 1994 until May 1998. It is photographed in company with LDV **J386DUG (1750073).** *P D Robinson*

Opposite, bottom:- **Iveco TurboDaily M736VSC (3750014)** photographed in 1995 when new It was built specially for the Laide to Achnasheen services by Mellor Coachcraft and includes a large mail locker. However, changes in the mail arrangements soon made this redundant. *P W Gumbrell*

1994

From April 1994 the products of the independent Leyland-DAF van company were rebadged as LDV, providing assorted 200s and 400s, including the first with three-point seat belts as a requirement of Strathclyde Regional Council for use on the school contract on Luing, while 4750003 had an Access wheelchair lift. One diesel-engined Peugeot 405GLX estate was purchased locally by Scotland, while a white Metrocab with Royal Mail cruciform logo was tried on at least one route in Scotland and inspected in the South East.

4750001-4750004	LDV Sherpa 400 15-seat postbus (Chorley conversion)	
	(♣ 12-seat with wheelchair space and Access wheelchair tail-lift)	
4750005-4750010	LDV Sherpa 200 10-seat postbus (Chorley conversion)	
4750011	LDV Sherpa 400 10-seat plus wheelchair postbus (Chorley conversion)	
4760001	Peugeot 405GLX 4-seat estate car postbus	

serial	registration	chassis no.	location	route	in	out
4750001	M381TYG	949003	Malton (15)	Malton-Foxholes	9/94	current
4750002	M722VWT	952572	Northallerton-NN36	Bedale-Hawes-Northallerton	3/95	current
4750003♣	M229WSG	953172	Linlithgow-LN7	Linlithgow-Blackness/Maddiston	4/95	current
4750004	M853TSF	953296	Luing	Isle of Luing	2/95	current
4750005	M171KEG	958290	Peterborough	Divisional Reserve	7/95	
			Great Yarmouth	Great Yarmouth-Flegg	3/97	
			St. Neots	Kimbolton-St. Neots	c1/98	
			Peterborough	reserve		10/98
			Holbeach	Holbeach Gedney Drove End	10/98	current
4750006	M570MTT	958003	Tenby-R1	reserve	7/95	current
4750007	N944JUA	957973	Hexham-20	Hexham-Kielder Village	4/96	current
4750008	M837AUG	957995	Driffield-27	Driffield-Skipsea	7/95	2/98
			Louth-GY58	Louth-Goulceby	2/98	current
4750009	N446CSG	958338	Barra	reserve	3/96	
			Port Glasgow	crewbus		current
4750010	N404NGC	958254	Dorking-855	Dorking-Ockley	6/96	current
4750011	N475JGK	957495	Haywards Heath-321	Haywards Heath-Balcombe	5/96	current
4760001	M709VSC	71331239	Melrose-MR4	Melrose-Maxton	1/95	4/98
			Aberfeldy	Aberfeldy-Glenlyon	4/98	current

LDV 400 N475JGK (4750011) has a power-operated side door as illustrated in this view at Balcombe.
P D Robinson

1995

LDV provided eight 200-series and five 400-series buses with varied seating but all having three-point harnesses. In addition when a vehicle was required at Morpeth the last numerically of the Leyland-DAF 400 crewbuses was sent to Chorley for conversion to postbus standard. An order for a single Peugeot 405 was cancelled and estate cars changed to the Ford Mondeo with an order for thirty delivered from mid 1995 to spring 1996. Four hundred Ford Courier Kombi four-seat crewbuses were introduced this year to take staff and mail out to their walks and Royal Mail South Wales & South West transferred one to postbus duties at Abergavenny when the subsidy was removed and another opened a new service from Whitchurch to Whixall. Another Defender 110 Station Wagon arrived fitted with a nearside passenger seat and a row of three behind, with the rear compartment to receive mail and other goods. It was intended to revive the Beauly to Cannich service, however support was not forthcoming from the Rural Development Commission and the vehicle was allocated elsewhere.

5750001-5750005	Leyland-DAF Sherpa 200 11-seat postbus	(Chorley conversion)
5750006-5750007	Leyland-DAF Sherpa 400 15-seat postbus	(Chorley conversion)
5750008-5750010	Leyland-DAF Sherpa 200 11-seat postbus	(Chorley conversion)
5750011-5750013	Leyland-DAF Sherpa 400 15-seat postbus	(Chorley conversion)
	(† 10-seat postbus with additional mail accommodation)	
5760002-5760031	Ford Mondeo Aspen 1.8TD 4-seat estate car postbus	
5770001	Land Rover Defender 110 Tdi 4-seat Station Wagon postbus	
5780816-5780823	LDV Sherpa 400 16-seat crewbus	(* 14-seat postbus Chorley conversion)
5890001-5890400	Ford Courier Kombi 4-seat personnel carrier	(+ postbus)

serial	registration	chassis no.	location	route	in	out
5750001	N401NGC	CN962423	Reigate-952	Reigate-Leigh	6/96	current
5750002	N402NGC	CN962801	Tunbridge Wells	Tunbridge Wells-Mayfield	6/96	current
5750003	N403NGC	CN962753	Canterbury-440	Canterbury-Crundale	6/96	current
5750004	N225GSC	CN962797	Lochboisdale	reserve	6/96	current
5750005	N226GSC	CN962757	Lochmaddy	Lochmaddy-Bayhead-Clachan	6/96	current
5750006	N447CSG	CN963602	Castlebay	Vatersay-Castlebay-Eoligarry	3/96	current
5750007	N575NAV	CN963627	Thetford	Holme Hale-Watton-Thetford	2/96	current
5750008	P58KSX	CN972428	Lochmaddy	Lochmaddy-Baleshare	9/96	
			Lairg	Talmine-Lairg	by 5/98	current
5750009	N947GSG	CN973632	Stornoway	reserve	7/96	current
5750010	N273NGK	CN973258	Maidstone-62	Maidstone-Stockett/Sutton Valence	8/96	
			Sittingbourne-341	Sittingbourne-Wormshill	11/97	current
5750011†	P59KSX	CN972768	Lochmaddy	Lochmaddy-Airport	9/96	
			Lochmaddy	Lochmaddy-Baleshare	by 5/98	current
5750012	N948GSG	CN973024	Stornoway	Timsgarry-Stornoway	7/96	current
5750013	P914EOM	CN973017	Lutterworth-53	Lutterworth-Peatling Parva	9/96	current
5760002	M587AEH	BBDNSC55414	Sedbergh	Sedbergh-Dent-Kendal	7/95	current
5760003	M702XSG	BBNSD39769	Skerray	Skerray-Tongue	7/95	current
5760004	N686DWY	GBBNSE00294	Louth-GY58	Louth-Goulceby	9/95	2/98
			Driffield-27	Driffield-Skipsea	2/98	
5760005	N464CSG	GBBNST47100	Applecross	Applecross-Toscaig-Torridon	11/95	
			Portree	reserve	3/97	current
5760006	N407CSG	GBBNTA92674	Dunvegan	Dunvegan-Glendale	4/96	current
5760007	N413CSG	GBBNTA92676	Beauly	Strathconon-Beauly	4/96	current
5760008	N414CSG	GBBNTA92665	Inverness	Inverness-Gorthleck	4/96	current
5760009	N415CSG	GBBNTA92666	Dingwall	Dingwall-Heights of Dochcarty	4/96	current
5760010	N408CSG	GBBNTA92662	Kyle of Lochalsh	Kyle-Plockton-Stromeferry	4/96	current

5760011	N409CSG	GBBNTA92673	Portree	Portree-Waternish	4/96	current
5760012	N410CSG	GBBNTA92671	Kyle of Lochalsh	Arnisdale-Kyle	4/96	current
5760013	N411CSG	GBBNTA92670	Kyle of Lochalsh	Kyle-Letterfearn	4/96	current
5760014	N412CSG	GBBNTA92668	Shieldaig	Shieldaig-Strathcarron-Toscaig	4/96	
			Poolewe	Poolewe-Cove	3/97	
			Lochgilphead (LG11)	Lochgilphead-Inveraray-Dalmally	-/98	current
5760015	N418CSG	GBBNTA92684	Lairg	Lairg-Altass	4/96	4/98
			Lairg		4/98	current
5760016	N451FSC	GBBNTA92672	Banchory	Banchory-Ballater/ Lumphanan	4/96	current
5760017	N436FSC	GBBNTA92669	Biggar (BG2)	Biggar-Abington-Crawfordjohn	4/96	current
5760018	N439FSC	GBBNTA92664	Castle Douglas-9	Castle Douglas-Corsock	4/96	current
5760019	N557FSC	GBBNTA92661	Lockerbie	reserve	5/96	current
5760020	N552FSC	GBBNTA92675	Lockerbie	Lockerbie-Corrie Common	4/96	current
5760021	N553FSC	GBBNTA92679	Lockerbie	Lockerbie-Waterbeck	4/96	current
5760022	N554FSC	GBBNTA92680	Annan	Annan-Creca	4/96	current
5760023	N558FSC	GBBNTA92667	Lockerbie-2	Lockerbie-Hightae	4/96	current
5760024	N452FSC	GBBNTA92708	Bettyhill	Bettyhill-Kinbrace	4/96	current
5760025	N453FSC	GBBNTA92683	Lochinver	Lochinver-Drumbeg	4/96	current
5760026	N454FSC	GBBNTA92682	Scourie	Scourie-Kylestrome	4/96	current
5760027	N455FSC	GBBNTA92681	Melvich	Armadale-Melvich-Thurso	4/96	current
5760028	N456FSC	GBBNTA92678	Sanday	Lady-Sanday	4/96	4/98
			Sanday	mailcars	4/98	current
5760029	N457FSC	GBBNTA92677	Sanday	Sanday-Stove	4/96	4/98
			Sanday	mailcars	4/98	current
5760030	N437FSC	GBBNTA92660	Dalmally	Bridge of Orchy-Dalmally	5/96	current
5760031	N438FSC	GBBNTA92663	Oban-OB13	reserve	5/96	current
5770001	N949GSG	988913	Dingwall	(awaiting allocation)	7/96	
			Pitlochry-PY11	Pitlochry-Dalnaspidal	2/97	current
5780823*	P177RYK	973199	Morpeth-4	Morpeth-Alwinton	9/96	current
5890151+	N343MUB	BAJ5TB21557	Moortown-MT117	crewbus	6/96	
			Hexham	Hexham-Slaley	by 5/98	by 5/98
			Hexham	crewbus	by 5/98	
5890268+	P678OEH	BAJ5TB21544	Northwich-NO17	crewbus	10/96	
			Whitchurch	Whitchurch-Whixall	11/97	
			Northwich	crewbus	6/98	current
5890331+	N172WTT	BAJ5TB09551	Brecon-BN22	crewbus	7/96	
			Abergavenny-A10	Abergavenny-Skenfrith	5/97	current

Opposite, top:- **The Kettletoft Arms is run by one of the two Postbus drivers on the Orkney island of Sanday and his wife. The Post Office, also run by his wife, is to one side and both the island's buses N456/7 FSC (5760028/9) are posed for the camera in front of it when new in August 1996.** *D A Cott*
Opposite, bottom:-
One of the three Ford Courier Kombi cars used as expedients on postbus work is P678 OEH (5890268) borrowed from Northwich to start the Whitchurch to Whixall service in November 1997. *P Eckersley*

Below:- **LDV 400 P177RYK (5780823) was ordered as a personnel carrier, a need arose for another large postbus during the changeover period to Pilot and Convoy production and it was sent from LDV at Washwood Heath to Chorley for conversion before entering service at Morpeth in September 1996. It is pictured at Rothbury in August 1997.** *D A Cott*

1996

In 1996 the Sherpa-derived LDV 200 and 400 models were facelifted as the Bulldog range, being launched as the Pilot and Convoy respectively. One Pilot 10-seater being ordered for the revived Chathill-Bamburgh service, while one more Pilot and two Convoys were ordered for new routes. Of the Convoys, 6750005 was reduced to 10 seats and having a large rear cage to carry bulk mail between the delivery offices of Dorchester and Bridport. The order for a further LDV Pilot for a new route in Anglia division was cancelled and serial number 6750006 was not used.

The main order was for fifty-nine Pilots and twenty Convoys, two of which were downseated to eight for Lochboisdale, together with another Pilot. Chorley closed in March 1997 when the lease expired and subsequent postbus conversion work has been carried out at the LDV factory. 6750003 was retained there for experiments with internal layouts after the bulkier forward-facing seats caused difficulties with passenger access and driver's rear view. Estate car deliveries again favoured the Ford Mondeo, with twenty-five, the first of which was intended for a projected service from Tunbridge Wells to Stonegate which failed to obtain funding from East Sussex County Council.

6750001	LDV Pilot 10-seat postbus (Chorley conversion)
6750002-6750003	LDV Pilot 10-seat postbus (LDV conversion)
6750004	LDV Convoy 15-seat postbus (LDV conversion)
6750005	LDV Convoy 10-seat postbus with mail compartment (LDV conversion)
6750007-6750065	LDV Pilot 10-seat postbus (LDV conversion) (♥ 7-seat plus mail or † 6-seat plus mail)
6750066-6750085	LDV Convoy 15-seat postbus (LDV conversion) (‡ 8-seat plus mail compartment)
6750086	LDV Pilot 9-seat postbus (LDV conversion)
6760001-6760025	Ford Mondeo Aspen 1.8TD 4-seat estate car postbus

serial	registration	chassis no.	location	route	in	out
6750001	P842 SWY	DN007154	Alnwick-33	Alnwick-Bamburgh	11/96	current
6750002	R759 XAV	DN010492	Saffron Walden (129)	Littlebury-Saffron Walden	10/97	current
6750003	R685 WOB	DN010702	St. Neots-SN21	Kimbolton-St. Neots/Covington	2/98	current
6750004	R895 GGO	DN010941	Ashford, Kent-903	Ashford-Biddenden	10/97	current
6750005	P206 ETA	DN015646	Dorchester	Dorchester-Bridport	6/97	current
6750007	P895 WGN	DN013600	Maidstone-24	Maidstone-Lenham Heath /		
				Sutton Valence	7/97	current
6750008	P630 NCR	DN014165	Newbury-NB2	Newbury-West Ilsley	6/97	current
6750009	P890 WGN	DN014481	Canterbury-459	Canterbury-Wootton	7/97	current
6750010	P335 YWT	DN014180	Alnwick-32	Alnwick-Wooler	7/97	current
6750011	P892 WGN	DN014455	Gravesend-GL25	Gravesend-Fairseat	7/97	current
6750012	P226 ETA	DN014419	Brecon	Brecon-Talgarth	7/97	current
6750013	P725 SMB	DN014228	Barrow-in-Furness	Broughton-Cockley Beck	7/97	current
6750014	P631 NCR	DN014213	Petersfield-P21	Froxfield-Petersfield	7/97	6/98
			Chippenham-PB3	Chippenham-Sopworth and		
				Melksham/Reading as 8-seater	10/98	current
6750015	P632 NCR	DN014507	Hungerford-HB1	Hungerford-Lambourn	7/97	current
6750016	P633 NCR	DN014237	Newbury-NB3	Newbury-Brightwalton	7/97	current
6750017	P726 SMB	DN014281	Ulverston	reserve	7/97	current
6750018	P634 NCR	DN014295	Swindon-PBR	reserve	7/97	current
6750019	P722 SMB	DN014303	Chester-C48	Chester-Tattenhall	7/97	current
6750020	P893 WGN	DN014342	Gravesend-GL26	Gravesend-Betsham	7/97	current
6750021	P721 SMB	DN014325	Ulverston	Ulverston-Grizedale Forest	6/97	current
6750022	P913 RSC	DN014418	Port Ellen	Port Askaig-Bowmore	6/97	current

6750023†	P494 OSC	DN014549	Lairg	Thurso-Wick Airport	6/97	current
6750024	P856 RSC	DN014353	Melrose-MR7	Galashiels-Melrose-Lilliesleaf	6/97	current
6750025	P914 RSC	DN014495	Port Ellen	Port Askaig-Port Ellen	6/97	current
6750026	P851 RSC	DN014599	Livingston-LV21	West Calder-Tarbrax	6/97	current
6750027	P852 RSC	DN014704	Edinburgh-DI3	(driver trainer)	6/97	current
6750028	P915 RSC	DN014593	Biggar-BG10	Biggar-Tweedsmuir/Lanark	6/97	current
6750029	P916 RSC	DN014691	Larkhall	Strathaven-Dungavel	6/97	current
6750030	P917 RSC	DN014605	Annan	Annan-Powfoot	6/97	current
6750031♥	P919 RSC	DN014573	Brodick-BK8	Arran (South) services	7/97	current
6750032	P854 RSC	DN014614	Hawick-HK16	Hawick-Bonchester Bridge	6/97	current
6750033	P918 RSC	DN014634	Thornhill	Thornhill-Moniave	6/97	current
6750034	P855 RSC	DN014725	Kelso-KO2	Kelso-Stichill	6/97	current
6750035	P853 RSC	DN014674	Kirriemuir F5 to K151	Kirriemuir-Glen Clova	6/97	current
6750036	P929 RSC	DN014797	Lochgilphead-LG11	Lochgilphead-Inveraray-Dalmally	7/97	4/98
			Newton Mearns-429	crewbus	5/98	current
6750037	P876 RSC	DN014726	Dundee F4R to R152	reserve	7/97	current
6750038	P862 RSC	DN014752	Aberfeldy-PY6	Aberfeldy-Lawers/Bridgend/Kenmore	7/97	current
6750039	P920 RSC	DN014738	Kirkcudbright	Kirkcudbright-Borgue	6/97	8/97
			Denny-DY24	Denny-Fintry	8/97	12/97
			Edinburgh-R9	reserve	7/98	current
6750040	P931 RSC	DN014904	Lockerbie-R	reserve	7/97	current
6750041	P921 RSC	DN015005	Port Ellen-PT10	reserve	6/97	current
6750042†	P495 OSC	DN014996	Alligin	Alligin-Kinlochewe-Achnasheen	6/97	current
6750043	P857 RSC	DN014818	Aberfeldy-PY5	Aberfeldy-Glen Lyon	6/97	4/98
6750044	P922 RSC	DN014802	Scarinish-SCA4	Isle of Tiree	6/97	
			Kirkintilloch-X165	crewbus	by 8/98	current
6750045	P858 RSC	DN014859	Cupar-CP1	Cupar-Peat Inn	6/97	4/98
6750046	P496 OSC	DN014852	Kyle of Lochalsh	reserve	6/97	current
6750047	P859 RSC	DN014916	Galashiels-GLR4	reserve	6/97	current
6750048	P863 RSC	DN014891	Haddington-HDB	Haddington-Garvald	7/97	current
6750049	P864 RSC	DN014902	Edinburgh-PBR	reserve	7/97	current
6750050	P932 RSC	DN015029	Lockerbie-3	Lockerbie-St. Anns	7/97	current
6750051	P865 RSC	DN015110	Glenrothes-FR4	Glenrothes R and Cupar-Newburgh	7/97	4/98
			Glenrothes-FR4	Glenrothes reserve	4/98	current
6750052	P923 RSC	DN014970	Castle Douglas-3	Castle Douglas-Mossdale	6/97	current
6750053	P924 RSC	DN014985	Biggar-BG12	Biggar-Newbigging	7/97	current
6750054	P860 RSC	DN015028	Dunbar-DB1	Dunbar-Innerwick	6/97	current
6750055	P925 RSC	DN015050	Lanark	reserve	7/97	current
6750056	P926 RSC	DN015126	Castle Douglas-13	Castle Douglas-Auchencairn	7/97	current
6750057	P110 SEW	DN015045	Dereham-DE103	Hingham/Welborne-Dereham	7/97	current
6750058	P927 RSC	DN015167	Port Ellen-PT9	Port Ellen-Portnahaven	9/97	current
6750059	P861 RSC	DN015105	Dalkeith-DAB	Dalkeith-Gorebridge-Moorfoot	6/97	current
6750060	P928 RSC	DN015112	Port Ellen-PT12	reserve	9/97	
			Leven-LE15	Leven-New Gilston	by 2/98	current
6750061	P883 RSC	DN015133	Grangemouth-R25	reserve	7/97	current
6750062	P731 SMB	DN015155	Llandrindod Wells-LD18		7/97	
			Aberystwyth	reserve		current
6750063	P732 SMB	DN015177	Llanidloes-LS8	Llanidloes-Llangurig	7/97	current
6750064	P733 SMB	DN015187	Llanidloes-LS7	Llanidloes-Dylife	7/97	current
6750065	P734 SMB	DN015203	Aberystwyth	Aberystwyth-Cwmystwyth	7/97	current

The larger LDV Convoy, like the Pilot model, has the asymmetric rear doors. P877RSC (6750084) operates as Killin-C21 on the service to Callander and is pictured there in April 1998.
P Walton

99

6750066	P894 WGN	DN014105	Sittingbourne-341	Sittingbourne-Wormshill	8/97	
			Maidstone-62	Maidstone-Stockett Lane	10/97	current
6750067	P899 WGN	DN014577	Maidstone-24	Maidstone-Lenham Heath/	10/97	
				Sutton Valence		
				Redhill-Outwood	12/97	current
6750068‡	P815 RSC	DN014422	Dingwall	reserve	7/97	9/97
			Lochboisdale	Lochboisdale-Balivanich	10/97	current
6750069‡	P816 RSC	DN014469	Laide	Laide-Achnasheen	7/97	9/97
			Lochboisdale	Lochboisdale-Benbecula Airport	10/97	current
6750070	P867 RSC	DN014492	Perth-R10	reserve	7/97	current
6750071	P868 RSC	DN014596	Grangemouth-R26	reserve	7/97	current
6750072	P869 RSC	DN014572	Denny-DY24	Denny-Fintry	7/97	8/97
			Kirkcudbright	Kirkcudbright-Borgue	8/97	current
6750073	P870 RSC	DN014642	Aberfoyle-AB11	Aberfoyle-Kinlochard	8/97	current
6750074	P871 RSC	DN014627	Callander-CL37	Callander-Trossachs	8/97	current
6750075	P872 RSC	DN014696	Aberfoyle-AB9	Aberfoyle-Inversnaid	8/97	current
6750076	P497 OSC	DN014747	Elgol	Elgol-Broadford	6/97	current
6750077	P817 RSC	DN014702	Tongue	Talmine-Tongue-Lairg	7/97	
			Lochmaddy	Lochmaddy-Airport	by 7/98	current
6750078	P818 RSC	DN014763	Lairg	reserve	7/97	current
6750079	P819 RSC	DN014759	Lochinver	Lochinver-Lairg	7/97	current
6750080	P820 RSC	DN014805	Durness	Durness-Lairg	7/97	current
6750081	P873 RSC	DN015347	Pitlochry-PY19	Pitlochry-Rannoch Station	7/97	current
6750082	P874 RSC	DN014822	Perth-R11	reserve	7/97	current
6750083	P875 RSC	DN014858	Crianlarich-C22	Killin-Crianlarich	8/97	current
6750084	P877 RSC	DN014881	Killin-C21	Killin-Callander	9/97	current
6750085	P930 RSC	DN014917	Dunoon-348	Dunoon-Tighnabruaich	7/97	current
6750086	P343 YWT	DN015683	Skipton-SK36	Skipton-Malham	7/97	current
6760001	R 34 JGK	GBBNTL28421	Rochester	Rochester-Cooling	10/97	current
6760002	P572 NSC	GBBNTT52574	Grantown on Spey	Grantown-Lochindorb	3/97	current
6760003	P573 NSC	GBBNTT52550	Nairn	Nairn-Glenferness	3/97	current
6760004	P574 NSC	GBBNTT52551	Invergordon	Invergordon-Kildermorie	3/97	current
6760005	P575 NSC	GBBNTT52552	Forres-F10	Forres-Braemoray	3/97	current
6760006	P576 NSC	GBBNTT52554	Huntly	Huntly-Lumsden	3/97	current
6760007	P438 NSC	GBBNTT52567	Balfron	Balfron-Fintry	3/97	current
6760008	P463 NSC	GBBNTT52565	Cupar-CP4	Cupar-Brunton	3/97	4/98
			Cupar-CP1	Cupar-Peat Inn	4/98	current
6760009	P464 NSC	GBBNTT52545	Hawick-HK15	Hawick-Craik	3/97	current
6760010	P465 NSC	GBBNTT52555	Duns-DS12	Duns-Abbey St. Bathans/		
				Cranshaws/Longformacus	3/97	current
6760011	P466 NSC	GBBNTT52557	Kelso-KO4	Kelso-Smailholm/Hassington	3/97	current
6760012	P577 NSC	GBBNTT52559	Kirkwall	reserve	3/97	current
6760013	P578 NSC	GBBNTL31943	Rousay	Isle of Rousay	3/97	current
6760014	P579 NSC	GBBNTT52553	Shieldaig	Shieldaig-Kishorn	3/97	current
6760015	P580 NSC	GBBNTT52562	Poolewe	Poolewe-Cove	2/97	
			Applecross	Applecross-Shieldaig	3/97	current
6760016	P581 NSC	GBBNTT52547	Kylesku	Scourie-Elphin	3/97	current
6760017	P582 NSC	GBBNTT52561	Kinbrace	Kinbrace-Melvich	2/97	4/98
			Scarinish	Isle of Tiree	4/98	current
6760018	P549 NSC	GBBNTT52546	Aros	Salen-Ulva Ferry/Berg	3/97	current
6760019	P550 NSC	GBBNTT52573	Tarbert-TB3	Tarbert-Skipness	3/97	current
6760020	P954 RGT	GBBNTT52570	Oxted	Oxted-Lingfield	2/97	current
6760021	P224 VUB	GBBNTT52569	Rothbury	Rothbury-Biddlestone	2/97	
			Morpeth-23	Morpeth-Whalton	by 8/97	current
6760022	P225 VUB	GBBNTT52568	Morpeth	Morpeth-Whalton	2/97	
			Rothbury-RB3	Rothbury-Biddlestone	by 8/97	current
6760023	P238 OMB	GBBNTT52563	Machynlleth	Machynlleth-Aberhosan	3/97	current
6760024	P667 CTA	GBBNTT52549	Narberth-N9	Narberth-Lawrenny	3/97	current
6760025	P583 NSC	GBBNTT23254	Gairloch	Gairloch-Redpoint	3/97	current

Opposite, top:- **The majority of the 1996 order for larger Postbuses went to Scotland, one of the few exceptions being P110SEW (6750057), which was used to inaugurate the two new routes from the Norfolk town of East Dereham. It is seen here in October 1997 between driver training trips, a week before entering revenue earning service.** *D A Cott*

Opposite, bottom:- **Deputising on the Aberystwyth-Blaenpennal route is reserve bus P731SMB (6750062) on a rainy day in September 1998.** *D A Cott*

1997

In 1997 no substantial orders have been placed, two vehicles being purchased for new services, an LDV Convoy (numbered to avoid the 1987 deliveries) and a Ford Mondeo estate car. The car was later displaced by a new Ford Courier Kombi crewbus, four of which were used as postbuses from new from the delivery of three hundred and forty-one, the other two displacing similar vehicles from 1995. Six Land Rover mailvans with postal serials were supplied early in 1998 and are included here for completeness.

7750003	LDV Convoy 15-seat postbus (LDV conversion)
7760001	Ford Mondeo TD 4-seat estate car postbus
7770001-7770006	Land Rover Defender 90 60cf. mailvan
7890001-7890341	Ford Courier Kombi 4-seat personnel carrier (+ postbus)

serial	registration	chassis no.	location	route	in	out
7750003	R714 UOP	DN024494	Great Yarmouth	Repps-Great Yarmouth	1/98	current
7760001	R730 FHT	GBBNVB35152	Hexham	Hexham-Slaley	10/97	
			Alnwick-31	Alnwick-Wooler-Kirknewton-Doddington	4/98	current
7770001	R541 HYG	143951	Halifax-HX31	mailvan	5/98	current
7770002	R269 AUX	144902	Llangollen-L6	mailvan	4/98	current
7770003	R348 GSX	143916	Craignure	mailvan	4/98	current
7770004	R542 HYG	143653	Halifax-HX32	mailvan	5/98	current
7770005	R349 GSX	143787	Bunessan	mailvan	4/98	current
7770006	R224 JSG	145324	Strathdon	mailvan	4/98	current
7890057+	R517 GNO	BAJ5WS74309	Hexham	Hexham-Slaley	4/98	current
7890177+	R421 GNO	BAJ5WS74996	Builth Wells	Builth Wells-Painscastle	4/98	current
7890338+	R289 GNO	BAJ5WS74283	Whitchurch	Whitchurch-Whixall	5/98	current
7890341+	R548 GNO	BAJ5WS74255	Llandrindod Wells	Llandrindod Wells-Llaithddu	4/98	current

A single Ford Mondeo TD estate car, R730FHT (7760001) was bought in 1997 and was initially used at Hexham until a Ford Courier Kombi was available and then moving to its intended route, the Alnwick-Wooler-Kirknewton-Doddington service. It is pictured in Wooler in April 1998. The Post Office now specifies new vehicles should be registered and taxed by manufacturer, bodybuilder or dealer, hence the unusual registration. *D. Longbottom*

1998

Towards the end of May 1998, following the stated intention to find a replacement for the ageing fleet of Land Rovers, a Vauxhall Brava 4x4 pick-up was purchased, having been taken on long-term loan in October 1997 and being tried on several Scottish services. It provided more comfortable passenger accommodation with four forward facing seats in a crew-cab with side doors and windows, while the mail was safely stowed under a Truckman hardtop over the loadspace. Orders were again placed with LDV for sixteen Pilots, the first seven being completed and awaiting Certification of Fitness as this book went to press, all destined for North Wales & North West Division. The rest are expected before Christmas, together with four Convoys. Estate car purchases reverted to Peugeot with fourteen of the revised 406 model purchased through Warwick-Wright of Chiswick, which were entering service in October 1998. S906NLM (8760014) was expected to be delivered to Stoke workshop to replace K630EYX (2750032) and allow one of the Stoke area services to be downsized to an estate car.

8110001	Vauxhall Brava 2.5TD pick-up postbus
8750001-8750007	LDV Pilot 9-seat postbus (LDV conversion)
8750008-8750016	LDV Pilot 9-seat postbus (LDV conversion)
8750017-8750020	LDV Convoy 14-seat postbus (LDV conversion)
8760001-8760014	Peugeot 406LXDT 4-seat estate car postbus

After trials on a number of routes in Scotland, Vauxhall Brava R64MWP (8110001) was purchased from White Arrow Express Ltd of Worcester and allocated to the Lairg-Durness route. As can be seen in this shot at Lairg station in August 1998, the extended crew-cab gives a row of passenger seats and the raised roof section behind allows for the many newspapers which are collected from the northbound train from Inverness for delivery along the route. *D A Cott*

serial	registration	chassis no.	location	route	in	out
8110001	R 64 MWP	9101497	Lairg	Lairg-Altnaharra-Durness	10/97	1/98
			Rogart	Rogart services	1/98	1/98
			Inverness	Inverness-Tomatin	2/98	2/98
			Blairgowrie	Glenshee and Glenisla services	4/98	
			Lairg	Lairg-Altnaharra-Durness	5/98	current
8750001	S391VJW	DN025023				
8750002	R778UOP	DN025247				
8750003	S392VJW	DN026140				
8750004	R620YOA	DN031448				
8750005	R621YOA	DN031598				
8750006	R622YOA	DN031713				
8750007	S487VJW	DN034847				
8750008						
8750009						
8750010						
8750011						
8750012						
8750013						
8750014						
8750015						
8750016						
8750017						
8750018						
8750019						
8750020						
8760001	S72NLN	80637193	Fort William	Fort William-Garvan	10/98	current
8760002	S915NLM	80637183	Newtonmore	Newtonmore-Kinlochlaggan	10/98	current
8760003	S977NLM	80637184	Aboyne	Aboyne-Logie Coldstone	10/98	current
8760004	S910NLM	80637188	Kelso-KO3	Kelso-Roxburgh	10/98	current
8760005	S902NLM	80637192	Bressay	Isle of Bressay	10/98	current
8760006	S37NLM	80637185	Kinross-K7	Kinross-Rumbling Bridge	10/98	current
8760007	S971NLM	80639394	Lismore	Isle of Lismore	10/98	current
8760008	S839NLM	80639392	Horesham	Horsham-Maplehurst	10/98	current
8760009	S962NLM	80639395	Machylleth	reserve	10/98	current
8760010	S903NLM	80640508	Brampton	Brampton-Castle Carrock/Alston	10/98	current
8760011	S833MRK	80637187	Dingwall	reserve	10/98	current
8760012	S973MRK	80637191	Alloa			
8760013	S813MRK	80637189	Ballachulish	Fort William-Glen Etive	10/98	current
8760014	S906NLM	80640509				

The latest deliveries, just as the book was in final preparation, involved the allocation of **Peugeot 406LXDT 4-seat estate cars. One of the first to be seen is 80639191 (S973MRK) pictured here.**

The Routes

In **1972** the trial period was complete and the GPO had become a publicly owned corporation independent of the Crown, The Post Office Act 1969 requiring it to provide an 'efficient and economic' postal service and specifically allowing it to 'carry for hire or reward passengers in the vehicles used by it for the purposes of its business'. The Act did not provide a duty to operate any sections of route not required for postal purposes but equally it did not prevent it. With the four experimental services considered successful, responsibility for Postbus operation was devolved to the Regional Headquarters provided that they conformed to three rules. The new services must not compete with existing bus routes, they must meet a clearly identified need for a bus service and most importantly they must fit in with and be consistent with overall postal obligations and unlike the contractor-operated services the mail has priority. A rural postman- or woman-driver will normally start work at the Delivery Office around 5am sorting the incoming mail, leaving before seven to make deliveries and empty boxes and returning by nine-thirty. On weekdays, some vans will have a second trip in the afternoon with a different driver to collect from the more important rural boxes therefore allowing a much quicker journey. To fit in with the mail requirements the typical Postbus service will not carry passengers on the circuitous early morning outward journey but will pick them up on the way back allowing several hours in the town before returning on the afternoon run. The long time taken on the outward run results from a large number of short delivery stops, and a few longer diversions which can be reduced with the agreement of the owners by delivering into secure boxes at the side of the road rather than to the houses. A few routes offer a better service by including a mid-day run allowing passengers to spend the morning, afternoon or all-day in the town. Some do not run at times when there are alternative services by other operators, while some routes in remote areas of Scotland have only one journey each day. Surveys have shown that the majority of Postbus passengers are women and retired people without the use of a car wanting to visit the town for shopping and personal reasons and that they are content with even the most basic service where none would otherwise exist. Some routes run mainly for tourists, those on the Scottish Islands co-ordinate with ferries, air services and even the tide, while a few offer fast town-to-town trunk services in the manner of Swiss Postbuses. The economic situation had also changed in favour of Postbuses - the new status of the Post Office made it eligible for the fifty per-cent New Bus Grant under the 1968 Transport Act, and bus fuel duty rebate, while the VAT regulations were changed to allow a greater recovery on the purchase of vehicles and fuel for buses than for mailvans. In addition the 1972 Local Government Act imposed duties on Counties to 'promote a co-ordinated and efficient system of public passenger transport' and where necessary to provide subsidies. Since the Post Office has to provide vehicles and drivers to fulfil its postal duties it is reasonable to consider only the additional cost of purchasing and running a small bus instead of a van, including higher capital and maintenance costs, administration, training and driver's wages. In 1973 the Post Office assessed the additional annual cost of running an 11-seat Postbus in place of a 50cf mailvan as between £250 and £300 per service, and most new services bettered that in fare receipts. Where routes were suitable for operation by estate cars or Land Rovers the small additional cost of PSV certification was easily outweighed by the various grants and rebates, albeit the potential for fares income is obviously limited.

Many decisions, such as the purchase of new vehicles, were made in London however the Regional Directors and Chairmen had some degree of autonomy in interpreting the rules for introducing Postbus services, which were far from clearly defined by The Post Office Act. Some Regions refused to alter mail operations in any way to suit passengers and avoided proposing services that might affect an existing bus service or which was not guaranteed a profit. Also, much management time was required for the slow process of negotiating with local authorities, applying for a full Stage Carriage Licence or Section 30 minibus permit and dealing with objections from existing operators. Two regions, however, saw that they could offer rural communities the benefit of a basic bus service and hopefully make a small profit in the process, most successful being the Scottish Postal Board under Director Trevor Carpenter and Operations Controller James Hall. They had enthusiasm, and what they lacked in bus operating experience was provided by the Highlands and Islands Development Board, and in particular its transport officer, Ken Cameron, who was able to weed out the non-starters and suggest some other routes to consider. Five new services were planned in Ross-shire, Sutherland and on the Western Isles, however before they commenced the existing service between Broadford and Elgol on the Isle of Skye was taken over from Lachlan MacKinnon when he retired, being combined with mailvan duties. The next service started in June that year between Lochmaddy on North Uist and the adjacent island of Benbecula, which had previously been operated by a MacBraynes bus with a mail compartment. There quickly followed routes in the Borders, Fife, Sutherland and on the Islands of Mull and Barra. The South Eastern Postal Region also took up Postbuses with enthusiasm, the first beginning at Canterbury in Kent in October 1972, and by the end of the year the number of services had risen to fourteen, of which ten were in Scotland, three in England and one in Wales.

1973 saw a further sixteen services commence in Scotland, mainly in the North West Highlands, but also one each in the counties of Nairn, Dumfries and Perth. The Lochinver to Drumbeg service which commenced in July had previously been operated by Hugh Matheson using a Bedford CA four-seater registered NS 4790. A network on Islay was taken over from Highland Omnibuses in October and an additional bus from November allowed considerable improvement in the services, linking with the Caledonian MacBrayne ferry and the British Airways flights at Glenegedale. Also in November the first Land Rover Postbus started a lightly loaded service over demanding terrain between Killilan and Dornie. In the South East two routes started at Dorking and Oxted in the Surrey commuter belt, less than twenty miles from the centre of London, while Midland Region began two routes at Billesdon in Leicestershire which were to run for only six years. At the end of the year the total was 35 of which 26 were in Scotland.

1974 saw increased growth with an additional twenty-seven services, seventeen of which were in various parts of Scotland including two more taken over from private operators: Stewart of Aberfeldy's service to Glen Lyon was acquired in January together with its Ford Transit, which was immediately replaced by a new Commer and sent to Rugby Management College. The Leyland Terrier thus released was sent to Islay where higher capacity was needed in the summer. A service started in October between Bonchester Bridge and Hawick that had been withdrawn by Anderson's at short notice in July. The South East introduced eight services including a network of three routes radiating from Hungerford, four in rural Sussex and another in Kent. A fourth service proposed at Hungerford was withdrawn after objections from local operator Swansdown Coaches. North Western Region added its second service, a scenic route in the Lake District while Eastern Region joined in with one on the Norfolk/Suffolk border.

1975 had a good start with another landmark service, the first to utilise a Morris Marina estate car on the lightly patronised route between Melrose and Maxton, followed quickly by another from Applecross to Toscaig, where loadings justified upgrading to a Bedford CF in June. Scotland's fiftieth service was achieved in March with a service from Dingwall to the Heights of Dochcarty. The Lairg to Atlass bus which commenced in September could be called the local taxi service as it was timed to meet the trains at Lairg station four times daily, and it was out unusually late in taking the outgoing mail to meet the 2015 train which normally brought in a number of passengers. On one memorable day in the summer of 1979 thirty-eight hikers appeared from the station wanting the bus to the village - the Marina and the reserve 11-seater made three trips to accommodate them and their backpacks. In October a service commenced between Arnisdale and Glenelg, previously operated by Lamont of Glenelg using an earlier series IIa Land Rover. In September Eastern Region commenced a service from Colchester to East Bergholt which replaced Eastern National route 77, but also that month proposals were abandoned for a service between Kirby Lonsdale and Newbiggin, and a proposed circular 'express' service between Leominster and Hatfield failed to start because three postmen were required to drive it and only one volunteered. East Sussex County Council called a meeting in April to review the first year of operation of the Mayfield service, running a free Postbus from Tunbridge Wells to the village for interested parties. The service had been more successful than anticipated, requiring a subsidy of around £40 instead of the £400 originally sought, and the Post Office agreed to several suggested improvements to the service, subject to approval by the Traffic Commissioners. The Sittingbourne to Wormshill service was extended to Bicknor in June but reverted to its earlier route in September due to lack of patronage. Until now the marginal cost of replacing a van with a Postbus was taken into account for subsidy purposes, however in 1975 the Post Office sought a revised cost formula to include general administration and driver training. In addition it requested West Sussex County Council to pay the £400 subsidy on an

A large number of Postbuses were ordered in 1975 and many were delivered before they were really required. TWO957S (5750041) was one of many stored by S.E.P.R. before it was reallocated to Wales and given bilingual lettering, eventually entering service at Usk in July 1978. *M J O'Sullivan*

E614CGM (6750014) operated at Hungerford until March 1992 and then passed to the Slough Post Office Sports & Social Club. It was photographed at Slough in January 1994. *P J Rogers*

existing service plus the anticipated £1500 loss on proposed services at Arundel and Storrington in advance, while in September proposals for a service between Brighton and Henfield, failed to materialise. Despite the set-backs a record thirty-three services were introduced in 1975 and by the end of the year the national total was 95.

1976 started with another important service between Laide and Achnasheen, a trunk run carrying bagged mail collected from sub-Post Offices en-route for transfer to the Inverness to Kyle of Lochalsh train at Achnasheen station and distributing incoming mail from the train, while at Kinlochewe there was a two-way exchange of mail with the Alligin Postbus. The service was taken over from Highland Omnibuses who had used a large bus, however the Post Office was prevented from running a similar vehicle as the regulations required that buses above 20-seat capacity have doors under the control of the driver and be operated by concerns with certificated managers, which it did not have. The service commenced with the former Highland driver using the downseated Leyland Terrier bus again seconded from Rugby, but its four-cylinder engine developed insufficient power to maintain the schedule on this difficult route and a larger six-cylinder Leyland Boxer was transferred from Cardiff. This had been a 44-seater so reducing it to 19 provided space for mail and the heavy goods traffic accepted from the railway. The route was very popular with tourists during the summer but it was later decided that a 16-seat Ford Transit reduced to eight seats could cope with the winter traffic and a second Transit could be used in the tourist season between Kinlochewe and Achnasheen, all fares being paid to the 'service' driver. Only a couple of weeks after Laide the century was reached with a service from Glenluce to Stranraer, commemorated by the chairman of Wigtown District Council handing over the keys of the new Commer which was adorned with a special plaque. The bus provided New Luce and several other villages with a connection to Stranraer, no postal work being carried out on that section and the costs were to be covered by the Council, however the patronage was so sparse that the service was reviewed after a few months and the route curtailed, and later downgraded to an estate car. A service commenced in February on the Isle of Colonsay which is connected at low tide to the smaller Isle of Oronsay by the Strand. The Land Rover Postbus meets the ferry from Oban, tours Colonsay then crosses to Oronsay and back in the afternoon, timings depending on the tide and sometimes requiring wading in a foot of salt water. The Isle of Luing received a service in May, well patronised by schoolchildren such that almost 26,000 passengers were carried in the first two years when a 16-seat Ford Transit was introduced to cope with the demand. In September the Post Office began operating a service between Henley-on-Thames and Frieth following the surrender of the licence by Alder Valley for its service 37 when Buckinghamshire County Council decided to reduce the subsidy. A Postbus Stop sign was erected in Henley Market Place, compulsory on the outward journey but request-only on the inward, and a diversion to the railway station would be made if required, while no boarding was allowed in either direction on the main road between Henley and Hambleden to avoid competing with other services.

1977 saw fewer new routes including a Wednesday-only service commenced in April from Kelso allowing an hour and a half at Peel Hospital using the Kelso to Stichill Commer, but no part of that service was covered. Less than five years after the first journey at Dunbar, Scotland launched its hundredth service with due celebration at Inveraray Castle on 6th May where the Duke of Argyll christened the Commer with Cruachan Whisky to the accompaniment of Pipe Major Ronnie McCallum, Seventeen days later Scotland's most heavily used route commenced from Killin to Callendar. During May the Dorking bus received a mention in the Daily Express as not only being the closest to London but also the most successful, showing a profit of £5 per week. The Abington to Crawfordjohn service was extended on Mondays and Fridays for passengers only to Lanark on a trial basis as part of the Department of the Environment's Rural Transport Experiment, RUTEX, which involved sixteen trials also including shared hire-cars, drivers of private cars charging fares, and variable-route minibuses. The Biggar to Newbigging service was extended to Carnwath in September in conjunction with a dial-and-ride service operated by Wilson's of Carnwath with a Bedford CF minibus named 'The Medwyn Gipsy' by local children. The Director of Eastern Postal Region, Gerry McMorran (who had introduced the Diss and Colchester services) reversed previous management apathy when he became Chairman of Wales and the Marches Postal Board. The first new Welsh service was also part of the RUTEX initiative and commenced at Llandovery in August, followed by the second in the South West in September and one at Rhyl in October. The end of August saw a network of three routes radiating from Brodick on Arran, to which a fourth was added the next year. There was strong local support for a postbus service from Kirkwall to Tingwall on Orkney, but the local operator was not prepared to surrender his licence. In these circumstances the Post Office was not prepared to proceed as it was policy to drop a proposal in the face of objection from an existing operator. This decision was particularly disappointing as the Post Office was prepared to operate the service at no cost to the taxpayer whereas the holder was drawing a subsidy. At that time the Scottish Postal Board Chairman, Trevor Carpenter, stated that in general Postbuses in Scotland operated without any financial support from local authorities, the main exceptions being where the authority requested the introduction of a new service or to extend an existing service over a route which was not strictly necessary for postal purposes. The Post Office was willing to do this if it was practicable and in such cases it was appropriate to cost the bus without offsetting the cost of the alternative mailvan. In all cases, however, the subsidy required was considerably less than that which would be required for a conventional bus service. In a development this year, Postbus drivers on the Isle of Wight began issuing Rover tickets, which had been valid on Postbuses for some time, and in return the Post Office received a share of the overall revenues. The scheme was extended later in the year to British Rail/Southern Vectis Breakaway Vouchers. The Glenluce to Stranraer service was the first to cease, in December, as changing mail traffic patterns would have required the subsidy from Wigtown Council to be doubled.

In February **1978** The Glenluce service was reinstated as far as New Luce using an estate car, the passenger-only section between New Luce and Stranraer being abandoned, while public support was also lacking for the RUTEX service to Lanark and it was withdrawn in March. In April the Post Office took over an existing service from Blairgowrie to the ski resort of Glenshee. The service was started by J. Harper & Sons of Blairgowrie with a 1949 Austin K8, later replaced by a 1962 Ford Thames Trader with seven seats and a rear mail compartment. This bus passed with the route to A. & C. McLennan in 1964 and a Ford Transit was purchased in 1972, which operated until the Post Office took over with a Commer, reduced to 7-seats by removal of the two inward facing seats and the rear double to accommodate the large volume of mail and goods. The Commer design was notorious for being front-heavy, the lack of traction in snow and ice on the Glenshee bus being solved by carrying several paving slabs in the rear loadspace, but the long-term solution was the use of a Land Rover. Three services commenced in Wales, Llandrindod Wells to Llaithddu at the end of June that has proved popular with tourists, and a pair out of Usk in July - both buses were displayed at Usk Agricultural Show in September leading to requests for more services but both have since ceased. In July a service between Dunoon and Tighnabruaich was taken over from Cowel Motor Services of Dunoon using a twenty-seat Bedford which often ran well loaded; thoughts of using the Achnasheen reserve Leyland Terrier on this service came to nothing and the Commer displaced from Glenluce was transferred in. Also in July a three-service network was introduced in Cupar using Avengers, however the Tuesday afternoon run to Newburgh was operated by a Commer. A strange service commenced on 28th September between Aberfeldy, Fearnan and Acharn, running once every fortnight on alternate Thursdays, initially authorised until 21st December it was extended into 1979 at the request of Tayside Regional Council, whose publicity leaflet surprisingly carried an outline of a modern double-decker with the slogan GO BY BUS. The Applecross to Toscaig service was extended to Shieldaig (where it exchanges mail with D. MacLennan's mail bus service from Strathcarron) in October on the opening of a new coast road, however the year finished with another closure, the unique evenings-only Durness to Rispond service which connected with the afternoon service from Altnaharra but suffered lack of patronage.

Scotland started **1979** with no unregistered buses in the pools for the first time in around five years, and began only three new services in the year, the most interesting being the 'long-haul' route from Talmine to Tongue and then thirty-seven miles to Lairg. This was basically another trunk route using a Transit downseated to ten to give space for mailbags, and meeting the Rispond Postbus at Altnaharra. The service had previously been operated by Sutherland Transport and Trading in two parts (Tongue-Talmine with a minibus and Altnaharra-Tongue with a conventional bus) until the company encountered financial difficulties and the mail contract was not renewed. There were also three new services in Wales and four in England of which probably the most surprising was Redhill to Outwood, just over twenty miles from central London. In November Reading's six services carried their fifty-thousandth passenger

The cover picture shows L48GOK(2750030) working the Leek to Wetton postbus service. Here is shown the rear of the Leyland-DAF 200, an advanced version of the Sherpa model. *Mark Skillen*

There was only one estate car Postbus ordered in 1994 - Peugeot 405 M709 VSC (4760001). It is seen here at Maxton Post Office in August 1997, about to return to its base at Melrose. *D A Cott*

who was presented with a year's free travel. Midland Region's only two services, at Billesdon, ceased in September the victims of competition from a Midland Red service introduced the previous year. The Leicester Head Postmaster said that he was pleased to have provided local customers with a bus service when there was no other, and that the two postmen-drivers would continue to provide local postal services. The two routes carried a total of 9,324 passengers in their six years, an average of around three passengers per day but the fares were extremely low flat fare of seven pence for an 80-minute round trip, requiring £1,310 from the County Council in the last year of subsidy. The solitary English Bedford spent some time working for the South Eastern Region Public Relations Office, and was repainted and re-seated (but not PSV licensed) to operate a special service on 18th July in connection with the International Year of the Child. Purchasers of the complete set of first day covers were treated to a twenty-minute return trip from Hartfield in East Sussex to Winnie the Pooh's bridge, which featured on one of the commemorative stamps. Proposals for a service in the Spilsby-Frisby area of Lincolnshire came to nothing. This year, Scottish Postbuses ran 2,272,168 miles and carried 156,162 passengers.

Half of the eight new services in **1980** were in Wales including a second at Llanidloes, the Aberystwyth route being shared with some journeys by David James and also partly covered by a Crosville service to Lampeter. Over the border in Shropshire the situation was not so favourable, with the public transport sub-committee of the County Council reluctantly agreeing to look into the feasibility of three possible services out of Craven Arms and one south of Bridgnorth, and to ask Midland Postal Board to consider altering the postal arrangements to suit, which proved impossible. In the South East, West Sussex County Council agreed to subsidise Petworth-Bignor for a further five years at a cost of £2500, while East Sussex suggested a route between Ninfield, Hooe and Battle after Maidstone & District withdrew their service to Bexhill. The three north of the border, two of which were in Orkney, were to be the last new Scottish routes for over two years. A planned service in Durham was abandoned when United Automobile Services heard of the proposals and re-routed a colliery service to cater the passengers, however another route commenced in the North East in May between Chathill and Bamburgh on the Northumbrian coast which proved popular from the outset, frequently requiring the driver to drop short-trip passengers and then double-back for the rest, prompting British Rail to congratulate the Post Office in trebling the number of passengers using Chathill station.

The beginning of **1981** saw all fare restrictions being removed from all Scottish services, and also the extension of the original service from Innerwick to Oldmanstocks, while Applecross-Toscaig which had started with an estate car before being upgraded to a minibus, was extended and gained a second vehicle. However there were no new routes in Scotland and three other services closed. News from Wales was a little better with a new service in the Elan Valley complimenting the existing one at Rhayader, but it was to last just over two years and little further progress was made in Wales after Director, Gerry McMorran retired in 1980. The Usk to Bettws Newydd route ceased and the proposal to use the displaced bus on an approved service from Abergavenny to Grosmont was stalled due to opposition by three farmers over the loss of their doorstep delivery. The only other new services were a pair at Wooler, while the midday run into Morpeth of the Rothbury-Alwinton service was opened to passengers in November.

In September, at the request of Berkshire Public Transport Co-ordination unit, the Newbury to West Ilsley service was extended to serve Farnborough for passengers only as it is in the adjacent Oxford postal area. The Stour Valley service ceased in April after the National Bus Company re-routed the Colchester to Ipswich service to compete. The Martindale bus, with no passengers on board, ran into a stone wall at Margate Cross on 18th May, and the driver, 44 year old John Hutchinson, died of natural causes later that day in Cumberland Infirmary.

1982 saw seven new services, including one from Clarkston to Carmunnock in the suburbs of Glasgow which was possibly the only truly urban Postbus route yet, it commenced in April but it has not survived. Two English routes started in 1982 have proved successful, including one at Reigate, on the fringe of London, which the villagers of Leigh requested when the local bus service was withdrawn, and that between Ripon and Masham. The latter co-ordinated with the Colsterdale Shared Car Service and United Automobile service 36 and was upgraded to a 14-seater in 1988. The Thurso to Wick Airport service introduced in November was basically a shuttle service for passengers, mail and newspapers from the Air Ecosse flights from Aberdeen and a flat fare of £1.95 was charged for the 20-mile trip. The spare Rhyl bus made trial runs over a proposed route between Capel Curig, Bettws-y-Coed and Llanrwst, on which Gwynedd County Council was offering an annual subsidy of £1000, however around ten residents refused to accept a roadside letterbox. Capel Curig Council asked for the names and addresses of the objectors in order to persuade them to agree. Sutherland Transport and Trading was in difficulties again at the end of the year when the Traffic Commissioners suspended the licences, suggesting that the Post Office take over the Durness and Lochinver mail bus routes, and Rapsons the Bonar Bridge service. Dodge 9750073 was despatched from Lockerbie to Lairg in December ready to take over, however ST&T appealed against the decision and was given three months to qualify for new licences, ruling out any immediate Post Office involvement.

In **1983** there were no services commenced or withdrawn, and a proposal by Devon County Council to support a service operated by Land Rover between Lynton and the Brendon Valley failed.

In **1984** the first route for eighteen months commenced in June between Builth Wells and Painscastle, it was planned for an estate car but commenced as a three-month trial with the redundant 11-seater from Rhyl to avoid capital outlay, and the need for a larger bus was proved from the first week. In contrast, the Meriadog service ceased, as did the Elan Valley, having carried only twenty five passengers in two years, and was replaced by a Social Car scheme. The other new service, Land Rover operated and covering a sparsely populated moorland, was Scotland's first for just under two years, replaced a bus, mail, milk and newspaper service run by John C. Keir of Glass. Two South Eastern routes closed, Heathfield to Waldron being replaced on market day by a Leyland Cub operated by Southdown, and two Scottish services ceased and two more amalgamated to save running costs.

In **1985** the Diss to Gislingham service ceased abruptly in June despite being well-patronised right to the end, carrying 60,000 passengers in its first five years and frequently requiring the reserve to duplicate or backtracking to pick up passengers left behind. The Petworth to Bignor route also closed, being replaced by a Voluntary Bus Association using a vehicle donated by the County Council. A special service was operated on 15th June 1985 from Shrewsbury station for an Open Day at Hookagate Long Rail Welding Depot as part of a nation-wide British Rail initiative. Two services started, both in Scotland - the second Land Rover service from Huntly delayed by driver training, and a hatchback service from Turriff that had been planned for seven years.

In February **1986** when Pitlessie Post Office closed temporarily a free service for customers was operated to the nearest alternative at Kingskettle, over 2 miles away, twice a week until July. The only proper service to commence this year was in Wales, between Aberystwyth and Cwmystwyth on a three month trial basis from July. The trial was successful with the bus running full on some days, and Dyfed County Council wanted it to continue but as no vehicle was then available a temporary contract was given to Jones of Tregaron to run it from the end of September. Deregulation of bus services under the 1985 Transport Act took place in October with services requiring a subsidy being put out to tender. The Tomatin to Coignafearn service was extended to Inverness in October, while the Lairg to Altass bus ceased serving Lairg railway station, this being operated by ST&T, while a service was proposed for Ellon but was deferred until after deregulation.

Late in **1987** two services started in Scotland, the Melvich to Thurso route effectively completing coverage of the former Highland Omnibuses mail route between Tongue and Thurso, while the Strathy service was extended to Melvich, and there we no closures.

In **1988** the planned service at Carbost on Skye, to be the fiftieth controlled by Inverness District, was postponed when the prospective driver failed the PSV medical, and the only new service this year was from Gairloch, although two services closed in Scotland, including Clarkston to Carmunnock in July The Henley to Frieth service ceased at Easter and the two troubled Isle of Wight routes in June, replaced by Southern Vectis with a new minibus service and an extension of an existing double-deck route.

January **1989** saw the take-over of the Mail Bus Service from James Duncan of Kinloch Rannoch whose minibus met the train at Rannoch station twice daily. The replacement Postbus service involved re-routing the mail via Pitlochry and used a three year old Sherpa released from the Public Relations fleet. A Maestro Postbus replaced the Glenisla Coaches 16-seater to Blairgowrie in June after the company requested a 150% increase in its fee for delivering mail, however the car lacked the space to carry crates of milk but a Sherpa was too large to reach isolated houses along the route. The first new route in England for seven years (and the first to use an estate car) commenced at Canterbury in May using a hired Toyota until the allotted Ford Sierra was available. The service was wholly subsidised by Kent County Council and introduced at their request when East Kent withdrew their twice weekly service to Stodmarsh. Ten Postbuses were used in the summer to give poor families from Glasgow a day at Butlins holiday camp at Ayr.

In March **1990** the Wensleydale service, between Leyburn and Hawes, was launched with much publicity, with three additional minibuses hired to transport the guests through 'James Heriot Country'. No Postbus services closed this year and another contract was absorbed in January when the Post Office took over the transport of mail between Ullapool and Achiltibuie that had been carried on Mrs MacKenzie's bus since 1959. Two Welsh Postbuses were used to transport visitors to the Courier Fun Day showground from Arley station on the Severn Valley Railway in May. During this period the future of Postbuses was uncertain as deregulation threatened to allow other operators to cream off passengers on profitable routes such as Ripon-Masham. In the event, National Bus Company subsidiaries tended to give up loss-making rural services rather than cross-subsidise them, leaving scope for the Post Office to take over. The subject was discussed at Board level and instead of the feared retrenchment, a Postbus Development Team was established based on the Finance Division at Chesterfield.

In **1991** the two-hundredth service started in April between Morpeth Whalton and Bolam, followed by one at Chester that had a passenger-only morning run which displayed a windscreen notice declaring its subsidy by Cheshire County Council. The next service, at Ballachulish, mirrored a licence application made in 1975 to replace a section of a Highland Omnibuses service abandoned when the new bridge was built, while two services ceased, at Usk and Wooler.

August **1992** saw the award to Royal Mail of two mail bus routes from Lairg previously operated by Sutherland Transport and Trading but since their demise by Rapson, who was so upset at losing them that he complained to the Office of Fair Trading. The objection was rejected because the services had been won by competitive tender, and in fact on the Lochinver service a third operator had also placed a lower bid. The round trip between Durness and Lairg was around one hundred miles, the longest yet. A new route in Scotland started in November, while the Chathill to Alnwick service was replaced in April by a new service between Wooler and Alnwick using the same vehicle.

1993 saw the first fruits of the new enthusiasm with twenty eight services started and none lost. The year began with two short afternoon services out of Penrith won in competitive tender, both worked by the Martindale bus after its normal duties, firstly over Cumberland service 105 to Greystoke Post Office (which continues), followed by a trip on service 106 which served Pooley Bridge and Glenridding Pier, which ended in May 1993. These were followed by the first services in Northern Ireland, at Enniskillen where two local routes fed the trunk service to Belfast Airport in the late afternoon. Two other local networks of three routes commenced at Stafford and Chippenham, where the Sunday collections are made by Postbus and then trunked along the A4 to Reading Mechanised Letter Office using one of the three buses. Kent County Council agreed to subsidise seven new services that commenced in May, some of which were in areas apparently well served by conventional buses. The two Wooler routes were amended in the summer and again in November to avoid disruption of the mail service in the area. Expansion of the Postbus services, whilst rapid when compared with previous years did not match expectations and in addition the shortage of crewbuses resulted in vehicles not immediately required for services being reallocated to staff duties, with the advantage that they could stand in as Postbus reserves when required.

1994 saw sixteen new routes around the country including one following the only road on the Isle of Lismore with timetable dependant on the arrival of the ferry, and a Wednesday-only on-demand service on Ulay for Strathclyde PTE which had to be booked twenty-four hours in advance. Another contract service was to transport two children from Milton of Campsie to Lennoxtown school and used the estate car rendered surplus at Brodick when the four Arran services were rationalised into two using larger buses, while the Aberystwyth to Aberffrwd bus followed different routes on alternate days. In August the mail ceased being carried by train to and from Achnasheen Junction and it was only a matter of time before the once-important Postbus service to Laide became unviable, however the Wensleydale service was extended to Northallerton where the mail was previously transferred by van. The Canterbury to Westmarsh route closed after eighteen months as it had seen few passengers and could not be downgraded to an estate car due to the volume of mail carried.

1995 saw five new services including two fully accessible buses on short routes, at Linlithgow and at Haywards Heath, the latter running only five miles to Balcombe. Despite deregulation nine years earlier the licence for the new Dent route prevented stopping between Kendal and Sedbergh and vice versa; incidentally the bulk mail was carried to Kendal on a Ribble bus until the late nineteen-eighties. Two Scottish Councils cut down on subsidies - Borders reduced support of Kelso to Roxburgh and withdrew completely from Kelso to Smailholm, while Dumfries and Galloway removed the subsidy from seven of their twelve routes, and several services were amended to cut costs. Only one service actually ceased this year, Alston to Nenthead.

1996 started with another odd service, the Biggar to Elsrickle circular operated afternoons only with the Tweedsmuir bus. The Hexham to Kielder Village bus in

Opposite, top:- **LDV Convoy P870RSC(6750073) is pictured outside the Aberfoyle Post Office in August 1997, about to work the Aberfoyle to Kinlochard service.** *P.D. Robinson*
Opposite, bottom:- **Reminiscent of the pulicity for 'charabanc trips' earlier in the century is this picture taken at Lairg rail station in August 1994. Of the seven routes out of Lairg, four used Sherpa and when the train was on time the passengers transferring to the postbuses would be taken the mile to the Post Office in one or two buses. However, when the train was late, up to three of the Sherpas meet the train, rejoining their routes directly from the station. Nearest the camera is J477FSR (1750068), the others being J305EST (0750114) and K242BSG (2750004) .** *D A Cott*

the Border Forest National Park was subsidised by Northumbrian Water and bore the company logo. The Alnwick to Alnham service closed in April after seventeen years without subsidy, however a new service commenced in November between Alnwick and Bamburgh, updating one which ceased in 1992. The other new route this year was at Thetford heralding an expansion of services in East Anglia. Co-ordination attempts by Western Isles Council saw the Lochmaddy services rationalised with different routes on different days, and the Barra service extended to Vatersay. New trunking arrangements in February to speed mail deliveries west of Lairg led to improvements in the connecting Postbus services, and only one service was lost - the Milton of Campsie service when the younger child left the school. Finally, a bold plan was announced to introduce the first Postbus into Inner London - from Richmond Station through Richmond Park to Kingston Gate; despite support from the Royal Parks Agency, sponsorship was not forthcoming for purchasing and running a wheelchair-compatible bus.

Early in **1997** Royal Mail Anglia commenced services at St. Neots and Saffron Walden before vehicles were available and so Postbuses were borrowed from existing services in order to use vehicles in the correct livery, being covered by hired vehicles. The trunk service connecting Dorchester and Bridport finally commenced in June more than twenty years after the idea was first discussed and replaced a Ford Transit on Southern National 73. In contrast the Littlebury to Saffron Walden service took just ten minutes, while the cost of providing a bus for the Dereham service was met by the Rural Development Commission and Norfolk County and the two District Councils provided a £6000 annual subsidy. The Stornoway services were re-arranged following Western Isles Council's co-ordination of passenger transport, and the Rhayader route extended to the popular Elan Valley Visitor Centre. The Biggar circular service, the Laide to Achnasheen trunk run, Denny to Fintry and two of the Canterbury routes ceased during the year, the last two being reintroduced the following spring after renegotiation with the County Council.

In **1998** The Labour Government's long awaited Transport White Paper was not published in time to prevent wholesale reductions in subsidies at the start of new financial year, such that fifteen services in Scotland and three in Kent were axed in April, while Hampshire County Council transferred the contract for the Petersfield to Froxfield service to Stagecoach. It was not all bad news, however, and the Builth Wells service continued with a smaller vehicle after the subsidy was removed, the Aberhosan route was extended to serve five more villages and the St. Neots bus was utilised on a Tuesday-only service to Covington. The White Paper announced, among other measures, the launch of a Rural Bus Partnership Fund with an additional £45 million per annum to improve rural transport, with Norfolk, Devon, North Yorkshire, Kent and Cornwall each receiving more than a million pounds of the first allocation. The Government's 'New Deal For Transport' whilst not specifically mentioning Postbuses, should promote a new period of growth with Rural Development Grants for new services in the South East were confirmed as this book went to press.

LIST OF POSTBUS ROUTES

Numbers in the following list are for reference only and are not used by the Post Office. Licensing of routes was undertaken by the regions until October 1986, then by the territories (Northern, Eastern and Western Letters Territory) and from April 1992, by the nine Royal Mail divisions. Routes operate Mondays to Saturdays unless shown otherwise.

No	Licence Holder	Service Name	Commenced	Ceased	Current Vehicle
1	W&BCPR	Llanidloes-Llangurig	20/2/67		
		revised to incorporate Wye Loop	2/10/67		6750063
2	S.W.P.R.	Honiton-Luppitt	23/10/67		2750033
3	N.W.P.R.	Penrith-Martindale	30/10/67		3750002
4	Scotland	Dunbar-Innerwick	4/6/68		6750054
5	Scotland	Elgol-Broadford	17/4/72		6750076
6	Scotland	Lochmaddy-Benbecula	16/6/72		6750077
7	Scotland	Lochmaddy-Solas-Newton			
		merged with Service 6	16/6/72	1/4/77	
8	Scotland	Castlebay-Airport-Eoligarry	17/8/72		5750006
9	Scotland	Melrose-Galashiels-Lilliesleaf	28/8/72		6750024
10	Scotland	Kylesku-Skiag Bridge-Elphin	15/9/72		
		revised as Scourie-Elphin	30/4/91		
		revised as Scourie-Elphin-Lochinver	5/2/96		6760016
11	S.E.P.R.	Canterbury-Crundale	23/10/72		5750003
12	Scotland	Craignure-Lochbuie	1/12/72	16/1/81	
13	Scotland	Tigharry-Lochmaddy	1/12/72		
		revised as Tigharry-Airport	1/4/77		
		revised as Bayhead via Sollas-Lochmaddy-Sidinish-Baleshare-Clachan	5/4/96		5750005
14	Scotland	Cupar-Peat Inn	4/12/72		6760008
14A	Scotland	Cupar-Newburgh via Letham (Tuesday afternoons)	1/8/78	4/4/98	
15	Scotland	Skerray-Tongue	29/1/73		
		revised as Skerray-Tongue-Melvich	27/10/86		5760003
16	Scotland	Nairn-Glenferness	28/2/73		6760003
17	Scotland	Lockerbie-St. Ann's	21/4/73		6750050
18	Scotland	Lockerbie-Hightae			
		merged with Service 91	23/4/73	12/4/78	
19	Scotland	Scourie-Laxford Bridge-Kylestrome	1/6/73		5760026
20	Scotland	Alligin-Kinlochewe	2/6/73		
		revised Diabaig-Achnasheen	30/5/94		6750042
21	Scotland	Strathconon-Muir of Ord	2/6/73		
		revised to Strathconon-Beauly	22/2/88		5760007
22	Scotland	Muir of Ord-Tomich (in conjunction with 21)	11/6/73	31/5/81	
23	Scotland	Lochinver-Drumbeg	2/7/73		5760025
24	Scotland	Ardgay-Strathoykel	21/7/73		2770026
25	S.E.P.R.	Dorking-Ockley	2/8/73		4750010
26	Scotland	Bettyhill-Kinbrace	10/8/73		5760024
27	Scotland	Biggar-Tweedsmuir	11/8/73		6750028
28	M.P.R.	Billesdon-Tilton/Lowesby (circular)	7/9/73	28/9/79	
29	M.P.R.	Billesdon-Rolleston/Illston (circular)	7/9/73	28/9/79	
30	S.E.P.R.	Oxted-Lingfield	24/9/73		6760020
31	Scotland	Thornhill-Moniaive	28/9/73		6750033
32	Scotland	Portnahaven-Port Ellen	1/10/73		6750082
33	Scotland	Port Askaig-Port Ellen - mornings	1/10/73		6750022
		afternoons	1/10/73		6750025
34	Scotland	Killilan-Dornie	7/11/73		
		revised to Kyle-Letterfearn	19/12/88		5760013
35	N.E.P.R.	Louth-Goulceby	7/11/73		4750008
36	Scotland	Anstruther-Arncroach	3/1/74	4/4/98	
37	Scotland	Aberfeldy-Lawers-Bridgend	3/1/74		
		revised to Aberfeldy-Killin	8/7/92		6750038
37A	Scotland	Aberfeldy-Kenmore (alternate Thursdays)	28/9/78		6750038
38	Scotland	Aberfeldy-Glenlyon-Lubreoch	3/1/74		4760001
39	N.W.P.B.	Broughton-Cockley Beck	1/3/74		
		also Broughton-Ulverston (Thursdays)	25/9/86		6750013
40	S.E.P.R.	Sittingbourne-Wormshill	4/3/74		
		revised as Sittingbourne-Wormshill-Bicknor	2/6/75		
		revised as Sittingbourne-Wormshill	8/9/75		5750010
41	S.E.P.R.	Petworth-Bignor	4/3/74	30/8/85	

One of the 1986 Ford Sierra postbuses was D981EFS (6760005) which operated the Cupar to Birkhill service from June 1987 to May 1992. It replaced Talbot Avenger A493WSD (1760001) which in turn had been brought in to replace accident-damaged KSF5X (0760035). P Walton

42	E.P.R.	Diss-Eye Gislingham	25/3/74	29/6/85	
43	S.E.P.R.	Tunbridge Wells-Wadhurst-Mayfield	1/4/74		5750002
44	S.E.P.R.	Heathfield-Waldron	3/6/74	1/12/84	
45	Scotland	Altnaharra-Portnacon	20/6/74		
		revised as Altnaharra-Rispond	9/9/75		
		revised as Durness-Altnaharra-Lairg	11/5/92		
		revised as Lairg-Altnaharra-Durness	5/2/96		8110001
46	Scotland	Tomatin-Coignafearn	20/6/74		
		revised to Inverness-Tomatin-Coignafearn	27/10/86		2770031
47	Scotland	Ardgay-The Craigs	20/6/74		2770029
48	Scotland	Haddington-Garvald	20/6/74		
		revised as Haddington-Stenton	2/11/98		6750048
49	S.E.P.R.	Hungerford-East Garston-Lambourn	2/7/74		6750015
50	S.E.P.R.	Hungerford-Great Shefford	2/7/74	26/9/81	
51	S.E.P.R.	Hungerford-Kintbury	2/7/74	-/11/91	
		Deregistered from 4/1/92			
52	Scotland	West Calder-Tarbrax	22/8/74		
		revised as Livingston-West Calder-Tarbrax	16/10/95		6750026
53	Scotland	West Linton-Romanno Bridge-Blyth Bridge	28/8/74		
		service suspended 2/76 - resumed 2/9/76			
		revised as West Linton-Drochill Castle	3/1/91		
		revised as Peebles-Drochill Castle	7/12/92	4/4/98	
54	Scotland	Castle Douglas-Corsock	29/8/74		5760018
55	Scotland	Castle Douglas-Mossdale	29/8/74		6750052
56	Scotland	Kirriemuir-Glen Clova	2/9/74		6750035
57	Scotland	Kirriemuir-Glen Prosen	2/9/74		2770016
58	S.E.P.R.	Hailsham-Bodle Street Green	19/9/74	14/9/84	
59	Scotland	Rogart-Scibercross	30/9/74		2770028
60	Scotland	Hawick-Bonchester Bridge-Southdeanrig	15/10/74		6750032
61	Scotland	Kelso-Nenthorn-Hume-Stichill	15/10/74		6750034

61A	Scotland	Kelso-Peel Hospital (Wednesday afternoons)	6/4/77	15/4/88	
62	Scotland	Portnahaven-Port Ellen (merged with service 32)	1/11/74	19/5/79	
63	Scotland	Melrose-Maxton	7/1/75	4/4/98	
64	Scotland	Aberfoyle-Kinlochard	8/1/75		6750073
65	S.E.P.R.	Newport (Isle of Wight)-Newtown	21/1/75	8/6/88	
66	S.E.P.R.	Newport (Isle of Wight)-Brighstone	21/1/75	8/6/88	
67	S.E.P.R.	Petersfield-Froxfield	11/2/75	27/6/98	
68	Scotland	Gorthleck-Killen Lodge		18/2/75	
		revised to Inverness-Gorthleck-Killen Lodge	8/6/87		5760008
69	Scotland	Applecross-Toscaig	27/2/75		
		revised as Applecross-Shieldaig	9/10/78		
		revised as Sheildaig-Applecross-Torridon	30/3/81		
		revised as Applecross-Toscaig-Torridon	27/3/95		6760015
69A	Scotland	Kishorn-Shieldaig	30/3/81		
		revised to Shieldaig-Strathcarron-Torridon	27/3/95		6760014
70	Scotland	Grantown-on-Spey-Lochindorb	4/3/75		6760002
71	Scotland	Selkirk-Ashkirk	7/3/75	4/4/98	
72	Scotland	Dingwall-Heights of Docharty	25/3/75		5760009
73	Scotland	Kelso-Roxburgh	25/3/75		8760004
74	Scotland	Leven-New Gilston	26/3/75		6750060
75	Scotland	Drumnadrochit-Grotaig-Achtermarack	26/5/75		0100082
76	Scotland	Castle Douglas-Auchencairn	6/6/75		6750056
77	S.E.P.R.	Newbury-West Ilsley	18/8/75		6750008
78	S.E.P.R.	Newbury-Brightwalton-Chaddleworth	18/8/75		6750016
79	E.P.R.	Colchester-East Bergholt	1/9/75	18/4/81	
80	Scotland	Durness-Rispond-Rhigoltar	9/9/75	30/12/78	
81	Scotland	Lairg-Altass		9/9/75	
		later Lairg-Altass-Rosehall	28/4/86	4/4/98	
82	Scotland	Plockton-Stromeferry	11/9/75		
		revised as Kyle-Plockton-Stromeferry	1/1/85		5760010
83	Scotland	Poolewe-Cove	12/9/75	4/4/98	
84	Scotland	Arnisdale-Glenelg	20/10/75		
		later Arnisdale-Kyle	17/4/78		5760012
85	Scotland	Locheport-Sidinish	27/10/75		
		revised as Lochmaddy-Sidinish-Baleshare	1/4/77	1/4/79	
		revised as Lochmaddy-Cheesebay-Sidinish-Baleshare-Grimsay-Tigharry-Lochmaddy	5/4/96		5750011
86	Scotland	Grimsay-Carinish	27/10/75		
		revised as Locheport-Grimsay	1/4/77	1/4/79	
87	Scotland	Melvich-Forsinard	3/11/75		
		later Kinbrace-Melvich	5/11/84	4/4/98	
88	Scotland	Dalwhinnie-Drummin	5/11/75		2770024
89	N.E.P.R.	Rothbury-Alwinton	11/11/75		5780823
90	Scotland	Annan-Powfoot-Cummertrees-Newbie	17/11/75		6750030
91	Scotland	Lockerbie-Hightae (afternoon service)	17/11/75		
		morning service transferred from service 18	12/4/78		5760023
92	Scotland	Lockerbie-Waterbeck	17/11/75		5760021
93	Scotland	Tarbert-Skipness	17/11/75		6760019
94	Scotland	Killin-Ardeonaig-Callander-Brig o'Turk	24/11/75		6750084
95	Scotland	Isle of Tiree	27/11/75		6760017
96	Scotland	Laide-Achnasheen	5/1/76		
		revised Dundonnel Hotel-Achnasheen	30/5/94		
		revised Braemore Junction-Achnasheen	15/8/94	27/9/97	
97	Scotland	Forres-Braemoray	19/1/76		6760005
98	Scotland	Lockerbie-Corrie Common-Millriggs	19/1/76		5760020
99	Scotland	Annan-Creca	19/1/76		5760022
100	Scotland	Glenluce-New Luce-Stranraer	20/1/76	10/12/77	
		reinstated as Glen Luce-New Luce	13/2/78	4/4/98	
101	Scotland	Aboyne-Logie Coldstone	26/1/76		8760003
102	Scotland	Invergarry-Kinlochourn	2/2/76		2770021
103	Scotland	Balfron-Fintry	9/2/76		6760007
104	Scotland	Isle of Colonsay	16/2/76		0100072
105	Scotland	Newtonmore-Kinlochlaggan	8/3/76		8760002
106	Scotland	Callander-Trossachs	30/3/76		6750074
107	Scotland	Aberfoyle-Inversnaid	21/4/76		6750075
108	Scotland	Isle of Luing	3/5/76		4750004
109	Scotland	Halkirk-Glutt-Altnabreac	19/7/76		2770030
110	Scotland	Biggar-Newbigging	16/8/76		6750053
111	S.E.P.R.	Henley on Thames-Frieth	20/9/76	31/3/88	

There is no reserve vehicle held to cover the Louth route if the postbus is off the road for maintenance. A replacement car is hired locally, but is not usually pcv tested - so fares cannot be charged. When Mondeo postbus N686DWY (5760005) was off the road for two months, with damage, green Vauxhall Vectra P722PWR, leased from K W Sadler Hire of Grimsby, was tested and carried the appropriate windscreen disc to prove it. *D A Cott*

112	Scotland	Dunblane-Braco-Langside	21/9/76		1770100
113	Scotland	Invergordon-Kildermorie	18/10/76		6760004
114	Scotland	Kirkcudbridght-Borgue	25/10/76		6750072
115	Scotland	Aberfeldy-Gilmerton-Birnam	25/10/76		
		revised as Birnam-Aberfeldy	10/2/79		1770104
116	Scotland	Hawick-Craik	15/11/76		6760009
117	Scotland	Pitlochry-Dalnaspidal	22/11/76		5770001
118	Scotland	Dollar-Glendevon	29/11/76		1770102
119	Scotland	Isle of Bressay	6/12/76		8760005
120	Scotland	Kelso-Smailholm	6/12/76		
		reduced to Tuesdays, Thursdays and Saturdays	4/6/84		6760011
121	Scotland	Kinross-Rumbling Bridge	7/2/77		8760006
122	Scotland	Abington-Crawfordjohn	22/3/77		
		revised to Biggar-Abington-Crawfordjohn	3/6/87		5760017
122A	Scotland	Abington-Lanark	24/10/77	31/3/78	
123	Scotland	Castlebay-Eoligarry via Borve(Barra)	1/4/77	24/4/94	
124	Scotland	Bernera-Callanish	4/4/77	6/4/96	
125	Scotland	Timsgarry-Callanish-(Stornoway Tu & Th)	5/4/77		
		revised as Brenish-Stornoway	6/4/96		5750012
126	Scotland	Huntly-Lumsden	2/5/77		6760006
127	Scotland	Inveraray-Drishaig-Dalmally	7/5/77		5760014
128	Scotland	Crianlarich-Killin-Callander	23/5/77		6750083
129	W.M.P.B.	Llandovery-Cilycwm-Rhandirmwyn-Myddfai	18/7/77		2750022

Opposite,top:- **The 1990 order for estate car Postbuses was split between Ford Sierras and Peugeot 405s. H647CST (0760029) replaced the Maestro car to serve the Orkney island of Rousay, where it was photographed in August 1996. It meets the morning ferry to collect the mail, allowing the small vehicles off before reversinging onto the ferry to shorten the distance the sack has to be carried from the crew's cabin to the tailgate.** *D A Cott*

Opposite, bottom:- **A further look at L48GOK, pictured in May 1995.** *Mark Skillen*

130	Scotland	Peebles-Manorhead	16/8/77	4/4/98	
131	Scotland	Duns-Abbey St. Bathans	18/8/77		
		reduced to Mondays, Wednesdays and Fridays	13/4/82		
		reduced to Wednesdays and Fridays	9/5/94		6760010
132	Scotland	Brodick-Shannochie	30/8/77		
		revised as South Arran circular	21/11/94		6750031
133	Scotland	Brodick-Blackwaterfoot	30/8/77		
		revised as North Arran circular	21/11/94		3750006
134	Scotland	Brodick-Pirnmill	31/8/77		9100116
135	Scotland	Biggar-Lanark (Mondays-Fridays) mornings	19/9/77		6750028
		afternoons			6750043
136	S.W.P.R.	Wadebridge-Penrose	20/9/77		1750043
137	W.M.P.B.	Rhyl-Meriadog	31/10/77	3/8/84	
138	Scotland	Brodick-Kilmory	16/1/78	29/8/94	
139	Scotland	Roy Bridge-Moy	6/3/78	28/7/84	
140	Scotland	Denny-Fintry	13/3/78	6/12/97	
141	Scotland	Bridge of Orchy-Dalmally	20/3/78		
		Dalmally-Bridge of Orchy	by 7/85		5760030
142	Scotland	Isle of Rousay	23/3/78		6760013
143	Scotland	Ballater-Linn of Dee	27/3/78		
		revised to Ballater-Glenshee	23/4/90		2770032
144	Scotland	Blairgowrie-Glenshee	1/4/78		2770015
145	Scotland	Strathaven-Dungavel	24/4/78		6750029
146	Scotland	Strathy-Strathy Point	5/6/78		
		revised to Melvich-Strathy-Strathy Point	14/10/87		
		(merged with 191)		13/2/89	
147	Scotland	Kelso-Hassington	5/6/78		
		(reduced to Mondays, Wednesdays and Fridays)	4/6/84		6760011
148	W.M.P.B.	Llandrindod Wells-Llaithddu	26/6/78		7890341
149	Scotland	Dunoon-Colintraive-Tighnabruaich	3/7/78		6750085
150	W.M.P.B.	Usk-Bettws Newydd	10/7/78	7/8/81	
151	W.M.P.B.	Usk-Llandenny-Llansoy	10/7/78	2/9/91	
152	Scotland	Cupar-Brunton	31/7/78	4/4/98	
153	Scotland	Cupar-Newburgh	31/7/78	4/4/98	
154	Scotland	Cupar-Birkhill	31/7/78	4/4/98	
155	Scotland	Dunvegan-Skinidin-Borreraig	27/11/78	31/8/81	
156	Scotland	Dunvegan-Glendale-Borreraig	27/11/78		5760006
157	Scotland	Gillen-Dunvegan-Waternish	27/11/78		
		revised to Portree-Waternish	18/12/95		5760011
158	Scotland	Linlithgow-Blackness	8/1/79		4750003
159	N.E.P.R.	Rothbury-Biddlestone	10/1/79		6760022
160	Scotland	Gorebridge-Moorfoot-Temple	26/3/79		
		revised to Dalkeith-Moorfoot-Temple	20/11/95		6750059
161	W.M.P.B.	Newtown-New Mills	4/6/79		2750010
162	N.W.P.R.	Ulverston-Grizedale Forest	4/6/79		6750021
163	N.E.P.R.	Alnwick-Alnham	10/7/79	30/3/96	
164	S.E.P.R.	Redhill-Outwood	1/10/79		6750067
165	W.M.P.B.	Builth Wells-Abergwesyn	12/11/79		2750011
166	W.M.P.B.	Machynlleth-Aberhosan	19/11/79		6760023
167	Scotland	Talmine-Tongue-Lairg	19/11/79		5750008
168	W.M.P.B.	Aberystwyth-Blaenpennal	7/1/80		2750007
169	Scotland	Kinross-Cleish	21/1/80	28/1/84	
170	Scotland	Sanday (Kettletoft)-Broughton	23/10/80	4/4/98	
171	Scotland	Lady-Rusness-Sanday	23/10/90	4/4/98	
172	W.M.P.B.	Abergavenny-Skenfrith	23/11/80		5890331
173	N.E.P.R.	Chathill-Bamburgh	12/5/80		
		revised as Chathill-Alnwick	7/10/91	25/4/92	
174	W.M.P.B.	Llandrindod-Wells-Rhayader(Mondays-Fridays)	19/5/80		2750016
175	W.M.P.B.	Llanidloes-Dylife	8/9/80		6750064
176	N.E.P.R.	Wooler-Donnington	10/8/81	1/4/91	
177	N.E.P.R.	Wooler-Kirknewton	10/8/81		
		revised as Wooler-Kirknewton-Donnington	1/4/91		
		revised as Alnwick-Wooler-Kirknewton	6/9/93		7760001
178	W.M.P.B.	Rhayader-Abergwngu	17/11/81	18/2/84	
179	N.E.P.R.	Ripon-Masham	24/3/82		2750040
180	Scotland	Clarkston-Carmunnock	26/4/82	25/7/88	
181	Scotland	Duns-Longformacus (Tuesdays, Thursdays, Sat)	13/4/82		
		reduced to Tuesdays and Thursdays	9/5/94		6760010
182	S.E.P.R.	Reigate-Leigh	6/7/82		5750001
183	Scotland	Banchory-Lumphanan	2/8/82		5760016
184	Scotland	Banchory-Ballater(Mondays-Fridays)	2/8/82	31/3/97	

The Postbus Handbook

Kenning Ford Transit long-wheelbase 14-seat minibus P874 AFV was hired by the Post Office in February 1998 to operate the Driffield to Skipsea service, in connection with an exchange of postbuses between the Driffield and Louth services. LDV M837AUG was transferred from Driffield to Louth in exchange for Mondeo N686DWY and the hired Ford Transit was used for about a week while the Mondeo was being prepared at Hull workshop. *D Longbottom*

185	Scotland	Thurso-Wick	22/11/82		
		reduced to Mondays-Fridays	29/11/88		6750023
186	W.M.P.B.	Builth Wells-Painscastle	4/6/84		7890177
187	Scotland	Huntly-Cabrach	8/10/84		2770019
188	Scotland	Huntly-Clatt	7/1/85		2770017
189	Scotland	Turriff-Woodhead-Fyvie	3/6/85	6/12/88	
190	W.M.P.B.	Aberystwyth-Cwmystwyth (Tuesdays-Saturdays)	1/7/86	27/9/86	
		reinstated as Mondays-Saturdays	3/9/90		6750065
191	NLT	Melvich-Thurso	14/10/87		
		revised as Armadale-Melvich-Thurso	13/2/89		5760027
192	NLT	Rogart-Muie & W Langwell-Lairg	18/11/87		2770022
193	NLT	Gairloch-Melvaig-Redpoint	19/9/88		6760025
194	NLT	Pitlochry-Rannoch Station	4/1/89		6750081
195	NLT	Canisbay-John O'Groats-Wick	30/1/89		2760010
196	ELT	Canterbury-Grove	15/5/89	6/4/97	
		service reinstated	14/4/97	15/4/98	
197	NLT	Blairgowrie-Glenisla	5/6/89		1770105
198	NLT	Invergarry-Fort Augustus	19/6/89		2770021
199	NLT	Leyburn-Hawes-Bedale (Mondays-Fridays)	6/3/90		
		revised as Northallerton-Hawes-Bedale	25/4/94		
		introduced on Saturday	22/05/95		4750002
200	NLT	Morpeth-Whalton-Bolam	2/4/91		6760021
201	WLT	Chester-Tattenhall (Mondays-Fridays)	23/9/91		6750019
202	NLT	Ballachulish-Fort William-Glen Etive	7/10/91		
		revised to Fort William-Glen Etive	5/9/84		8760013
203	RMNE	Wooler-Alnwick-Eglingham	26/4/92		6750010
204	RMS & NI	Durness-Lairg	10/8/92		6750080
205	RMS & NI	Lochinver-Lairg		10/8/92	
		revised as Drumbeg-Lochinver-Lairg	5/4/93		6750079
206	RMS & NI	Fort William-Garvan	2/11/92		8760001
207	RMNW&NW	Penrith-Greystoke (Mondays-Fridays)	4/1/93		3750002
208	RMS & NI	Maguiresbridge-Enniskillen	9/2/93		2750006
209	RMS & NI	Enniskillen-Belfast Airport	9/2/93		2750006
210	RMSE	Canterbury-Westmarsh	4/5/93	10/12/94	
211	RMSE	Canterbury-Marshside	4/5/93	6/4/97	
		Service reinstated	14/4/97	15/4/98	
212	RMSE	Canterbury-Wootton	4/5/93		6750009
213	RMSE	Sittingbourne-Hartlip	4/5/93	15/4/98	
214	RMSE	Rochester-Cooling	4/5/93		6760001
215	RMSE	Gravesend-Fairseat (Mondays-Fridays)	4/5/93		6750011
216	RMSE	Gravesend-Betsham (Mondays-Fridays)	4/5/93		6750020

217	RMSE	Maidstone-Stockbury Village (Mondays-Fridays)	4/5/93		
		extended to Hartlip Village on Mondays and Thurs	1/7/98		6750066
218	RMSE	Maidstone-Lenham Heath (Mondays-Fridays)	4/5/93		6750007
219	RMSE	Maidstone-Stockett Lane (Mondays-Fridays)	4/5/93		
		Tuesdays, Wednesdays and Fridays			6750066
		Mondays and Thursdays			2750020
220	RMSE	Maidstone-Sutton Valence (Mondays-Fridays)	4/5/93		6750007
221	RMNE	Skipton-Malham (Mondays-Fridays)	1/6/93		6750086
222	RMM	Stafford-Knighton (Mondays-Fridays)	21/6/93		2750023
223	RMM	Stafford-Millmeece (Mondays-Fridays)	21/6/93		2750032
224	RMM	Eccleshall-Stafford (Mondays-Fridays)	21/6/93		2750019
225	RMNW&NW	Alston-Nenthead	16/7/93	10/6/95	
226	RMNW&NW	Welshpool-Foel	26/7/93		
		reduced to Mondays-Fridays	11/4/94		2750018
227	RMSC	Chippenham-Lyneham (Mondays-Saturdays)	13/9/93		2750012
		Sundays			2750003
228	RMSC	Chippenham-Sopworth (Mondays-Saturdays)	13/9/93		6750014
		Sundays			2750012
229	RMSC	Chippenham-North Wraxall	13/9/93		2750003
230	RMSC	Chippenham-Melksham (Sundays)	19/9/93		6750014
231	RMSC	Chippenham-Reading (Sundays)	19/9/93		6750014
232	RMNW&NW	Crewe-Middlewich (Mondays-Fridays)	27/9/93		2750021
233	RMA ♣	Lutterworth-Peatling Parva	18/10/93		5750013
234	RMS & NI	Inveraray-Lochgilphead	20/12/93		
		Lochgilphead-Inveraray	28/12/95		5760014
235	RMNW&NW	Brampton-Castle Carrock-Alston	4/1/94		8760010
236	RMS & NI	Duns-Cranshaws (Mondays and Saturdays)	9/5/94		6760010
237	RMSE	Horsham-Maplehurst	31/5/94		8760008
238	RMSE	Ashford(Kent)-Biddenden	13/6/94		6750004
239	RMS & NI	Isle of Lismore	13/6/94		8760007
240	RMM	Rugeley-Abbots Bromley (Mondays-Fridays)	20/6/94		2750025
241	RMM	Leek-Hartington-Wetton (Mondays-Fridays)	11/7/94		2750030
242	RMA	Saffron Walden-U Langley-Clavering (Mon-Fri)	1/8/94		
		Introduced on Saturdays	31/5/95		3750018
243	RMS & NI	Kirkintilloch-Lennoxtown (schooldays)	17/8/94	9/2/96	
244	RMNW&NW	Aberystwyth-Aberffrwd	5/9/94		2750035
245	RMNE	Malton-Foxholes	5/9/94		4750001
246	RMSW&SW	Pembroke Dock-Angle	3/10/94		2750031
247	RMSW&SW	Pembroke Dock-Bosherston	3/10/94		2750028
248	RMSW&SW	Narberth-Landshipping	31/10/94		2750029
249	RMSW&SW	Narberth-Lawrenny	31/10/94		6760024
250	RMA	Ware-Buntingford-Sandon (Mondays-Fridays)	22/11/94		3750008
251	RMS & NI	Linlithgow-Whitecross-Maddiston (Mondays-Fridays)	23/1/95		4750003
252	RMSE	Haywards Heath-Balcombe	14/3/95		4750011
253	RMNW&NW	Sedbergh-Dent-Kendal	3/7/95		5760002
254	RMNE	Driffield-Skipsea	24/7/95		5760004
255	RMS & NI	Salen-Ulva Ferry/Burg	21/8/95		6760018
256	RMS & NI	Biggar-Elsrickle (Mondays-Fridays)	4/1/96	28/3/97	
257	RMA	Holme Hale-Watton-Thetford (Mondays-Fridays)	4/3/96		5750007
258	RMNE	Hexham-Kielder Village	15/4/96		4750007
259	RMNE	Alnwick-Bamburgh	18/11/96		6750001
260	RMA	Kimbolton-St. Neots (Mondays-Fridays)	3/3/97		
		(discontinued on Tuesdays)	14/4/98		6750003
261	RMA	Repps-Great Yarmouth	17/3/97		7750003
262	RMSW&SW	Brecon-Talgarth	28/4/97		6750012
263	RMA	Littlebury-Saffron Walden (Mondays-Fridays)	19/5/97		6750002
264	RMSW&SW	Dorchester-Bridport	23/6/97		6750005
265	RMS & NI	Lochboisdale-Balivanich	13/10/97		6750068
266	RMA	Hingham-Dereham(Mondays-Thursdays)	20/10/97		6750057
267	RMNE	Hexham-Slaley	20/10/97		7890057
268	RMA	Welborne-Dereham (Fridays)	24/10/97		6750057
269	RMNW&NW	Whitchurch-Whixall (Mondays-Fridays)	3/11/97		7890338
270	RMA	Covington-St. Neots (Tuesdays only)	14/4/98		6750003
271	RMSE	Canterbury-Grove (Mondays-Fridays)	27/7/98		hired
272	RMS & NI	Kirkcudbright-Twynholm (Wednesdays and Fridays)	29/9/98		6750072
273	RMA	Holbeach-Godney Drove End (Mondays-Fridays)	26/10/98		4750005
274	RMS & NI	Haddington-Humbie (Mondays-Fridays)	2/11/98		6750048

♣ Although an RMM service, the licence was applied for and is held by RMA as it operates in the Eastern Traffic Area.

The Postbus Handbook

There was only one Land Rover Postbus ordered in 1995. Delivered at N949GSG (5770001) it was intended for a new route from Beauly to Cannich. It was supplied to Dingwall workshop and stored, having had the unique route lettering applied beneath the windscreen. The expected subsidies and funding were not forthcoming and the vehicle was allocated to the Pitlochry-Dalnaspidal route the following year. *D A Cott*

For 1996 the estate car deliveries again favoured the Ford Mondeo, with twenty-five being supplied. Ford Mondeo P224 VUB (6760021) is seen at Morpeth in April 1998. From here the vehicle is used on the service to Whalton. *D Longbottom*

Tickets and Other Printed Material

No study of postbuses and the services they fulfil would be complete without some consideration of the many different types of tickets issued over more than thirty years, as well as other collectable printed material, such as timetables, faretables and maps, leaflets and posters, commemorative covers, picture postcards (issued by Royal Mail itself and from other sources) and photographs, special handstamps, postmark slogans and cachets marking first days in service and anniversaries.

Philatelists first began to be interested in postbus services in the early 1970s when different types of ticket came into use, mainly pre-printed stock in set values on coloured paper, or stamped cards with different values of postage stamps paying the fare, cancelled by means of named and sometimes dated handstamps. As the number of services steadily grew, postal historians were attracted to the challenge of getting hold of these items, usually available only by personal visit or contact, and by the regional autonomy that allowed such variety of design. A little later the Post Office Regions started issuing sets of postcards, many of which depicted postbuses amid attractive rural scenery.

It is not possible in this short chapter to do full justice to the extraordinary range of printed material available, and the best course is probably to indicate briefly region by region what type of tickets have been issued and to mention a few examples of the other items which have been produced to meet operational needs or satisfy collectors' demand.

Along with the three other experimental routes which began in 1967-68, the Llanidloes-Llangurig route in Wales at first used a second-hand TIM ticket-printing machine, believed to have been purchased from Bolton Corporation, which is now in the collection of the National Postal Museum. This became obsolete with decimalisation in 1971 and an Almex machine with serial number 0004 was introduced, but from 26th February 1979 this was replaced by white card tickets with bilingual heading, crossed posthorns printed in red and spaces for up to three stamps to be affixed to pay the (newly restructured) fares. The stamps were cancelled in black by an undated self-inking rubber handstamp 'BWS Y POST BRENHINOL/ROYAL MAIL BUS/LLANIDLOES-LLANGURIG'

On the first day of these new tickets a dated handstamp was used, inscribed bilingually 'First British Postbus/First Day of Issue', and this can also be found used as a cachet on mail posted locally on that day. It became usual on Welsh routes for there to be a special commemorative handstamp on the first day, and thereafter an undated mark showing the route. All the marks, and the tickets themselves, were bilingual.

From 1989, Almex machines, purchased from Yorkshire Rider, were widely used throughout Great Britain, but in 1994 two new services in Dyfed pioneered a new type of serially-numbered card ticket with rates from 5p to £5 and a "first day of service" star.

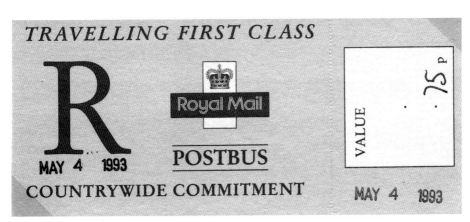

Above: **Kent printed return ticket with fare value in manuscript.**

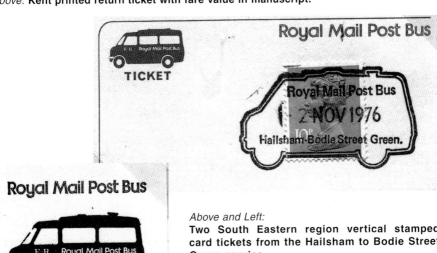

Above and Left:
Two South Eastern region vertical stamped card tickets from the Hailsham to Bodie Street Green service.

Below: **Bell Punch omnibus ticket from the Canterbury to Crundale service.**

No 0001

5_p	10_p
20_p	30_p
40_p	50_p
60_p	70_p
80_p	90_p
£1	£2
CONCESSIONARY	
SINGLE	RETURN

Left: **Self-Carbonating paper ticket from Ware to Buntingford service.**

POSTBUS
WARE

SERVING THE COMMUNITY

Left: **Eastern region titled ticket with crossed posthorns from the Colchester to East Bergholt service.**

Below centre: **Bell Punch roll ticket headed TRANSPORT SERVICES from the Louth to Goulceby service.**

Below right: **Billesdon card ticket.**

Post Bus

POST OFFICE
20p
0483

15772 Fb

TRANSPORT SERVICES

Issued subject to the bye-laws and regulations NOT TRANSFERABLE

ORD. W. RET.

Bell Punch Co. Ltd., London

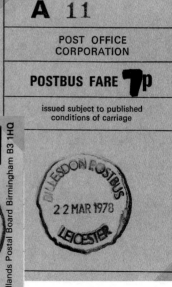

A 11

POST OFFICE
CORPORATION

POSTBUS FARE **7**p

issued subject to published
conditions of carriage

Royal Mail
Post
Bus
Fare 7p.

Issued subject to published conditions of carriage

Midlands Postal Board Birmingham B3 1HQ

Left: **Later Billesdon card ticket.**

The Postbus Handbook

In north-west England, the original Penrith to Martindale service used printed roll tickets from TIM, Almex and then Setright machines, while the Duddon Valley (Broughton-in-Furness) and Grizedale Forest (Ulverston) services used printed cards in a range of values and colours, which had to be changed and extended as fares rose. Originally each service had its own tickets, but they unified as Northern Territory from November 1986. Almex machines were used on later services, as in other regions.

Most South Eastern region services used standard small white cards with the silhouette of a Bedford postbus in red and space for postage stamps to be affixed to the value of the fare paid, which was cancelled by means of dated handstamp identifying the route. The tickets were originally vertical in format but from 1976 a horizontal design was introduced as new stocks were needed. Specialists distinguish several different types, the earlier ones now being exceedingly scarce. The rubber stamps used on the tickets were rectangular, oval or in the shape of a postbus, and usually struck in black, red or violet. Among these it is worth mentioning an example from the Tunbridge Wells-Wadhurst-Mayfield route dated 11 June 1985 with the clear mis-spelling TUNBIRDGE WELLS. The only service not to use these tickets at the time was the original Canterbury to Crundale route which, at first, issued a set of coloured Bell Punch Company omnibus tickets, then used a Setright machine.

It was possible to buy return tickets on the routes controlled by Head Postmaster Reading; these were indicated by an additional rectangular cachet on the rear with the service number, a large letter R and the words: 'VALID ON DAY OF ISSUE ONLY'. Although there is not enough space here to go into all the details of later tickets, it is perhaps just worth mentioning a couple of unusual ones From May 1977 Rover tickets for Southern Vectis buses and British Rail trains on the Isle of Wight became available for use on the island's two postbuses and special tickets were printed. Probably the oddest ticket is in the form of a small map, a souvenir of a special postbus journey to Poohs Sticks Bridge near Hartfield, East Sussex, on the day of issue of the Year of the Child stamps in July 1979. From 1993 printed tickets with fare values entered in manuscript by drivers were used on new services in Kent, and in the same year South Central services based at Chippenham used self-carbonating paper tickets.

In the south-west, the Honiton to Luppitt service has used a variety of printed paper tickets and stamped cards while Wadebridge to Treburrick originally had stamped tickets similar to those used in the south-east of England. They survived until April 1992 and were the last in the country to use postage stamps

The first service in the North Eastern region, Louth to Goulceby, used Bell Punch omnibus tickets from its inauguration in 1973 until they were replaced in 1977 by cards with space for four stamps to be affixed and cancelled by a rubber stamp with the route name and outline of a postbus. Other services used similar card (later paper) tickets in booklet form with the stubs retained for accounting purposes, until all were replaced by Almex tickets.

In the Midland region, two postbuses operated from Billesdon and a variety of printed card tickets were used, with a flat rate fare which rose from five pence to

The Royal Mail Anglia reserve postbus is based at Peterborough and M171KEG (4750005) is photographed at its base in May 1996. *M D Street*

seven pence. The tickets were cancelled by a rubber handstamp, each bus having a slightly different version. The services in the Eastern region, Diss to Gislingham and Stour Valley (Colchester to East Bergholt), used pre-printed tickets with a crossed posthorns motif, then Setright machine tickets. More recent services have used self-carbonating printed paper tickets bearing the route or divisional name.

After a brief experiment with printed card tickets on the Thornhill to Moniaive route in Dumfries & Galloway, from 1974 Scotland's postbuses used pre-printed roll tickets similar to those commonly found in many other applications. These were printed by the Glasgow Numerical Printing Company although the name did not appear on the first printings, which simply bore a 3-digit serial number and the value. From 1976 tickets carried the GNP Co Ltd (later GNP-Booth) imprint and were headed SCOTTISH POSTBUS SERVICES. Some remained in use alongside later Setright and Almex tickets. Northern Ireland services use Almex tickets.

As far as other printed material is concerned, most routes have individual timetable/faretables, sometimes incorporating maps. Occasionally leaflets and posters have been produced to publicise the inauguration of new or revised services. Since 1973 Royal Mail has published every year or two the current timetables collected together in booklet form. The latest 1998 timetable come in a set of twelve attractively produced booklets covering England, Wales, Scotland and Northern Ireland

The 1970s and early 1980s saw an immense growth of interest in picture postcards issued by regions, and the South East region was the most active in this respect, issuing some 68 cards between 1972 and 1986. Of these nearly half featured postbuses. It is impossible to mention all the postbus cards which have been issued, so some of the South East ones can serve as examples. The first card to be issued marked the inauguration of the Dorking to Ockley service on 2nd August 1973; there was also a souvenir cover and special handstamp. The Oxted to Lingfield service was also commemorated in 1973 and Canterbury to Crundale in 1974. Eleven further cards issued between 1974 and 1979 showed the postbuses at Sittingbourne, Tunbridge Wells, Hungerford, Newbury, Henley-on-Thames and Redhill. The Hungerford one, showing the postbus at Denford Mill House, had an unusual special handstamp in the shape of a postbus with the wording 'POST BUSES/ARRIVE IN BERKSHIRE/1 JULY 1974/HUNGERFORD, BERKSHIRE'. Some of the cards marking the Redhill to Outwood service had an additional printed cachet reading: 'Posted on first/day of Redhill-/Outwood Post Bus'. The high point was reached in 1980 when SEPR issued two sets of nine cards, all devoted to postbuses, the first showing services in Kent and Hampshire and the second those in Berkshire, Oxfordshire and Surrey.

The introduction of a bus with tail-lift conversion at Sittingbourne in January 1992 was marked by a limited edition card and handstamp sponsored by Royal Mail Canterbury. A caption on the reverse of the card reads: 'Representing Royal Mail commitment to the community, the Sittingbourne to Wormshill postbus shown overleaf is the first in the UK to be specially adapted to carry wheelchair passengers. All monies raised from the sale of this limited edition postcard will go towards the British Paralympic Team'. Postbus cards were also issued by the former Eastern, North Western, South Western, Scotland and Wales & The Marches regions, and are listed in such publications as Collect Post Office Cards, published by Rosendale Stamps Ltd.

K241BSG (2750005) is seen heading for Durness on the service to which it was allocated for some five years. The vehicle is a 14-seat conversion undertaken at Bamber Bridge. *D A Cott*

Commemorative covers and special handstamps sometimes mark the inauguration of a new service or the anniversary of an established one Slogans used in postmark machines are much less common. The 25th anniversary of Scottish postbus services was commemorated in 1992 by means of a slogan postmark 'TWENTY-FIVE YEARS OF SERVICE TO SCOTLAND 1968-1993 POSTBUS SILVER JUBILEE', This was used at Edinburgh, Glasgow and Perth from 5th July 1993 to 31st January 1994 (to 31st December 1993 at Perth), and another celebrating twenty-one years of postbus partnership with Northumberland County Council was used at Newcastle upon Tyne for one week only in November 1996 There are two versions showing a solid and outline postbus Cachets have often been used: sometimes rubber handstamps for cancelling tickets used on collectors' covers, or specially-printed ones such as:- POSTED ON THE ROYAL MAIL BUS; 'PENRITH TO MARTINDALE' in 1974; 'ROYAL MAIL SE POSTBUS OPERATIONS; POSTED ON THE POST BUS; CANTERBURY CRUNDALE/23 OCTOBER 1997/25 YEARS OF SERVICE'

This book is the work of the Post Office Vehicle Club, an enthusiast society dedicated to all aspects of road transport operation by the GPO, and its successors the Post Office and British Telecom.

The Club was formed to bring together people interested in current operations and vehicle purchases, and this interest remains to this day. In addition, it encourages the preservation of Royal Mail vehicles and a large number of preserved vehicles are owned by members of the Club. The Post Office has made over a significant amount of historic data on GPO vehicles and this information is being incorporated in the Club's historic records, with a view to producing a detailed history of GPO Motor Transport.

For more information on the Post Office Vehicle Club, please contact the Secretary at:- POST OFFICE VEHICLE CLUB , 7 Bignal Rand Drive, Wells, Somerset, BA5 2EU